Rosalind Scott

AWEIGH WITH MY MOTHER-IN-LAW!

Adventures afloat and ashore with the world's most infuriating passenger

Illustrated by Martin Regan

Rosalind Scott

AWEIGH WITH MY MOTHER-IN-LAW!

Adventures afloat and ashore with the world's most infuriating passenger

Illustrated by Martin Regan

MEREO
Cirencester

Mereo Books

1A The Wool Market Dyer Street Cirencester Gloucestershire GL7 2PR
An imprint of Memoirs Publishing www.mereobooks.com

Aweigh with my mother-in-law!: 978-1-86151-685-5

First published in Great Britain in 2016
by Mereo Books, an imprint of Memoirs Publishing

Copyright ©2016

Rosalind Scott has asserted her right under the Copyright Designs and Patents Act 1988 to be identified as the author of this work.

A CIP catalogue record for this book is available from the British Library.

This book is sold subject to the condition that it shall not by way of trade or otherwise be lent, resold, hired out or otherwise circulated without the publisher's prior consent in any form of binding or cover, other than that in which it is published and without a similar condition, including this condition being imposed on the subsequent purchaser.

The address for Memoirs Publishing Group Limited can be found at
www.memoirspublishing.com

The Memoirs Publishing Group Ltd Reg. No. 7834348

The Memoirs Publishing Group supports both The Forest Stewardship Council® (FSC®) and the PEFC® leading international forest-certification organisations. Our books carrying both the FSC label and the PEFC® and are printed on FSC®-certified paper. FSC® is the only forest-certification scheme supported by the leading environmental organisations including Greenpeace. Our paper procurement policy can be found at www.memoirspublishing.com/environment

Typeset in 11/16pt Century Schoolbook
by Wiltshire Associates Publisher Services Ltd. Printed and bound in Great Britain
by Printondemand-Worldwide, Peterborough PE2 6XD

PREFACE

I admitted murdering my late mother-in-law long before she died. I always said that if she was found strangled one day, it would have been by me. I even told my doctor, ready for him to vouch for my mental state at the time, whenever that should be, and in order not to waste police time or public money, I also told a friend or two... or three.

She probably died at her home on a Sunday evening; Alice-across-the-road noticed lights not switched off and curtains not pulled. She phoned Tracy-next-door, who found Mum dead the following morning. She had had a heart attack and would have known nothing about it. Poor Tracy, she was the best neighbour Mum could have had. What a shock, what a payback. For the rest of us, thank goodness she died like that. She would have hated being in hospital or a home, and they would have hated having her.

I have no alibi for that particular Sunday afternoon, evening or night, or Monday morning, for that matter. I was at home with Peter, my husband, over 60 miles away, but a husband cannot be an alibi for his wife, can he?

We will never know what precipitated the heart attack.

CONTENTS

Acknowledgements
About the author

1	We are asked to try the water	P.1
2	We dip our toes in It	P.5
3	Knee deep	P.10
4	In over our heads	P.12
5	Roll call	P.17
6	Pack Up Your Troubles	P.23
7	Alarm and excursion	P.26
8	Travelling Bud Lite	P.30
9	A timely tumble	P.36
10	And the baggage went round and round	P.39
11	Contraband	P.42
12	Water music	P.45
13	Finding the lifeboat	P.48
14	Sent to walk the plank	P.55
15	Becoming delusional	P.57
16	A bit of a hiccup	P.61
17	I-Spy	P.64
18	Adrift	P.70
19	Almost overboard	P.73
20	Our lives in our hands	P.80
21	The bugs begin to bite	P.85
22	The cakewalk, or is it the gangplank?	P.91
23	Sea's rough	P.95
24	Too much of the drink	P.100
25	Mum can't wait	P.104

26	Wet briefs at dawn	P.108
27	A fishy story	P.111
28	Mum visits the crow's nest	P.116
29	Water sports	P.121
30	Flotsam and jetsam	P.126
31	Maelstrom	P.130
32	The Titanic – an alternative version	P.136
33	The Foghorn	P.139
34	Thought reading	P.142
35	Bingo	P.145
36	Military precision	P.149
37	Message in a bottle	P.158
38	Let out of the bag	P.162
39	Watching the birdie and nearly missing the boat	P.167
40	Peter dances the hornpipe	P.170
41	Coming full circle	P.176
42	Picky eaters	P.179
43	Just ordinary	P.182
44	Dragons	P.187
45	Kitted out – or not	P.196
46	Battle of the South Pacific	P.199
47	Getting crafty	P.204
48	Inanimate objects	P.209
49	More inanimate objects	P.213
50	Not fleet enough	P.215
51	Water, water everywhere	P.223
52	There's many a slip	P.227
53	Food for thought	P.235
54	Gulls, wasps and other irritating creatures	P.242
55	Aristocratic Anastasia	P.246
56	A cautionary tale	P.252
57	Don't forget the water	P.254
58	Another cautionary tale	P.258
59	The Knowledge of the Ancient Mariner	P.261
60	Of sardines, snappers and a great white shark	P.264
61	Exodus	P.274

Dedicated to the most infuriating
person I have ever met

Lilian Florence (Maidment) Scott

10 March 1920 – 14 April 2014

Fondly remembered

ACKNOWLEDGEMENTS

Thanks must go to the following:

My husband Peter, who stopped me throttling my mother-in-law and Lilian from gouging out my eyes for over 45 years.

Lilian, for unwittingly supplying the material for this book.

Other cruisers, for adding the extras.

Friends who encouraged me to write this book.

Martin, for his inspired cartoons.

Trevor, for helping with the computer.

All at Mereo Books, particularly Chris Newton for his sympathetic editing and advice.

All the cruise lines we have ever travelled with, particularly Saga and Fred. Olsen Cruise Lines.

Lastly, the Royal National Lifeboat Institute (RNLI) for their fantastic work and bravery. This book is written for them, and all proceeds made will be donated to them.

ABOUT THE AUTHOR

With nothing else to do at the age of five, Rosalind Scott entered the education system, attending three eponymous holy schools, Bishop Winnington-Ingram in Ruislip, St Mary's Grammar School in Northwood and Bishop Otter College in Chichester, and achieving complete mediocrity at each educational stage. Since her leaving, each establishment, eager to sever all links with her, has attained witness protection status, and has either moved or changed its name. Her educational pinnacle was reached when her M Ed from Oxford Polytechnic became an MA from Oxford Brookes University; the latter was so keen to alter its image after she left that it made the change between her handing in her dissertation and graduating.

Unable to have children of her own, she borrowed everyone else's, inflicting on them her own unique style of education, and when they couldn't stand it any more, she advised and eventually inspected other teachers. The highlight of her career was crowning the May Queen at Silverstone, when the original choice was hit by a bug and Rose was the only person available at 24 hours' notice.

On reaching the mandatory age of parole, Rose received a bus pass and decided that this was a hint that she should keep on moving round the UK and the rest of the world. Her husband Peter has left home regularly on cruise ships to escape to the other side of the planet, only to find Rose has followed him. She lives with him at 'Tadpole Nursery' in Buckinghamshire, surrounded by a plethora of fish, frogs, spiders and birds.

ABOUT THE ILLUSTRATOR

Martin Regan was educated at Our Lady of Mount Carmel, Toxteth, and Netherley Comprehensive Schools, Liverpool. Not content to merely change their names, both establishments have since closed and been demolished. Martin went on the study Fine Art, both at Liverpool and Manchester Polytechnics, before qualifying as a teacher. He has since obtained an MA degree from Liverpool John Moores University, and taught art at a Catholic comprehensive school on the Wirral, Merseyside, for many years.

Some of the events in the following saga may have been tweaked just a little, in order not to bore the reader, but they are all based on real events. Some names have been changed in order to protect the writer.

1

WE ARE ASKED TO TRY THE WATER

'I've been thinking', my mother-in-law said.

Not a good combination, Mum and thought. Don't get me wrong, she could think all she liked, she was entitled to do that – let's face it, there is probably an EU directive about it. It was the way she said it. When thinking involved telling us about it, that's when the combination was lethal.

Peter was sitting in Dad's seat, on one side of her, and I was on the sofa on the other. We looked at each other, Peter and I. We knew what was coming. It would involve us intimately, and it wouldn't be good.

'As you, know, Dad died in August', she continued.

It was now November and we were hardly likely to have forgotten; one does tend to remember the passing of one's parent, or parent-in-law. It hurts, and it hurts for a long time. Dad was a gentleman, and much missed, but he couldn't deal with Mum when she wanted something. Before Dad, her parents indulged her, so we were not going to fare much better.

'Dad and I liked cruising,' she went on. Yes, we knew that too. Dad had wanted to go to all sorts of exciting places, but Mum only liked Europe, though not Italy as she didn't like Italian food, and not the new Europe, you know, the countries in the east, Hungary, Romania and Bulgaria. The Greek islands were fine, but the mainland was to be avoided, Turkey was out and anywhere without a coastline, or the UK, as that wasn't a proper destination at all. Apart from that, Europe was acceptable, so Mum and Dad went to her version of Europe.

'A brochure came from Trekkers yesterday, and I have been looking at it,' she said. The strategically-placed open Trekkers catalogue had not escaped our attention. 'I'm only interested in a ship called *Candy*, but I want to go on a cruise and I can't go on my own.'

'Have you asked your friends? Someone would probably jump at the chance to go with you,' Peter suggested reasonably. Peter is always reasonable. 'Winnie, for example.' Winnie was Mum's best friend and even more reasonable than Peter. Let's face it, she had to be.

'No one will come with me' Mum responded quickly, too quickly – we could immediately tell she hadn't asked anyone, and had no intention of doing so – 'and anyway, they can't afford it. No, there is a short cruise, a taster cruise they call it, and I want to go and I want you to come with me. I'll pay.'

The words were tumbling out now, as Mum described what she had already worked out. Picking up the brochure, she began describing a short cruise around the English Channel, just four nights.

Peter and I listened, in horrified silence. Five days and four nights with my mother-in-law? She could wind me up in that number of minutes and had done so from day one. Her feelings were always abundantly clear about everything, and she didn't approve of me. She tried to stop Peter seeing me, and when that didn't work, she dispatched Dad to send the same message. Then she refused to call me by my Christian name or my preferred short name of Rose. She called me 'Roslin' throughout her life (not that I have anything against that name, it just isn't mine). Never Rosalind, never Rose, despite Peter having introduced me as Rose.

Peter and I didn't dare look at each other. He was already ploughing through Mum's mountain of post and had changed two lightbulbs and three batteries, opened a couple of tricky bottles, rescued two Biros from behind the sofa and found 23p and three peanuts under the chair and we had only been at the house for twenty minutes. His head was down, totally absorbed in some junk mail which had suddenly become incredibly fascinating.

'I'll pay for it all,' she repeated earnestly. She did think if she threw money at a problem it would go away, and if she threw it at a person, they would do whatever she wanted.

'I've got lots of money.' We had heard that before, too.

Mum was 80, we were both 54. We wanted to turn her down flat, but it did seem cruel without at least giving it a go. Eventually, we agreed, with the proviso that if it didn't work, we wouldn't do it again, and Peter and I would do the deciding.

So that's it, that's how we climbed onto the roundabout that was cruising with my mother-in-law. Of course, after our taster, we had to agree to cruise again, a week this time, and then a fortnight and so on. She had hooked us and reeled us in, and there was no way out. Except that this was not a good simile. Far from getting out of the water, we were dropping into it.

2

WE DIP OUR TOES IN IT

'You have to get on the first coach' Mum told us the first night of the taster. We were at a table for eight, and most had never cruised before.

'Why?' Came the response from a chap from Morecambe, his brow furrowed in puzzlement.

'Well, it just is,' Mum replied, clearly having no ready answer to a perfectly reasonable question. Mum always did everything first or early; even when Peter was small and all his friends had lunch at 1 pm, he always had to come home to lunch at 12 noon. Invariably, he forgot to leave on time, and his host would receive a phone call summoning him home, the host always assuring Mum that Peter was already on his way. Lunch would be on the table at 12, no matter whether Peter was there to eat it or not.

'You must get to the show lounge early, so you can get a ticket for the first coach, or I'll get it for you if you like,' she concluded. She was assured that that would not be necessary and that everyone would be at the front of the queue, and with that we left the table for the first night of entertainment.

With at least half an hour to spare, we arrived in the lounge the following morning and all our table companions were already there. We sat there, seven virgins and Mum, who immediately organised us into giving her our excursion tickets so she could collect the coach tickets for all of us. Except they weren't just coach tickets, this was Guernsey and we were tendering and needed a tender ticket as well as a coach ticket. (Tendering is when the ship cannot draw right up to a berth for some reason, and has to wait out at sea with the anchor down so the passengers go ashore in lifeboats, called tenders). The Trekkers staff didn't make it easy either for themselves, or for us.

We sat for ages, repeatedly running to the loo, 'just in case'. Suddenly, the tour was called and mayhem erupted. Mum, along with just about everyone else, jumped up and barged her way to the front of the scrum for tickets, all elbows, knees and feet; they were all used in trampling over anyone in the way. We couldn't look; the staff were completely engulfed in a heaving mass of eighty-somethings acting like four-year-olds, with Mum just as bad as anyone. Worse than some.

'I did it!' she announced triumphantly on her return, holding up the tender tickets. 'We are all on tender one and coach one.' Then she gave out the tickets like Lady Bountiful.

Some minutes and several trips to the loo later, Tender One was called to the gangway. We had swipe cards which had to be shown and put away so we could use two hands to balance on the gangway, which was moving up and down at an alarming rate. We managed this somewhat slowly, and the tender gradually filled. We squeezed in and shoved up in order that we could all have a seat, and the tender set off.

Engulfed in exhaust fumes, we sat like a class of kindergarten children. I could see Guernsey off on the horizon as we bounced up and down in the swell. Ten minutes later it didn't seem any closer. I don't know how long it took, it seemed half a lifetime, but eventually we arrived at the jetty and thankfully transferred to a coach. We had a lovely drive round the island, stopping for tea and biscuits half way. It was great, we were on our own, no long queue for the ladies', plenty of seats and tea and biscuits to spare. We had thought we would meet another group going round the island the other way, but no. We boarded again and finished out trip.

Back at the jetty, things looked odd. On arrival,

there had been tea urns set up with parasols, bottles of water and eucalyptus towels, but coming back they had all disappeared, which seemed strange as we were the first coach out, so surely, the first coach back?

Someone in a hi-vis jacket began to shout at us as we approached the jetty. 'Come on, hurry up, everyone on the ship is waiting for you, get on board NOW!' Some of us began to run, some couldn't run, so they stumbled, tripped, fell, hobbled or shuffled back on the tender. The moment the last person was on and accounted for, we took off. Guernsey looked very close, but the *Candy* looked awfully far away. We bounced up and down, and up and down. We seemed to get no nearer. It was interminable.

Hi-vis jacket began to shout commands. 'As soon as we arrive at the ship, get to the exit, you can close your eyes if you like, just stand and we will pull you off in turn. When you arrive at the ladder, climb up as fast as you can, safely. Keep both hands on the rails. Get back on the ship, have your card ready to swipe and keep the gangway clear for the other passengers.'

What on earth was going on? We had had a dignified tour of Guernsey, but there was no dignity now. Back at the ship, we were pulled off the tender like peas out of a pod, and before we knew it we were all back on board, the tender was craned up and the *Candy* was on her way again.

At 12 noon, the ship's bell sounded and the captain spoke to us over the speaker system.

'I am so sorry you missed your tour of Guernsey today, but the swell was too dangerous to take out the tenders and we couldn't keep the ship in place as she was dragging her anchor. Those of you on the first (and only) tender were very, very lucky,' he said.

That evening we all met up again for dinner, the seven virgins and Mum. 'There you are,' she said triumphantly, a little smirk on her face (Mum couldn't ever smile properly). 'I told you the first coach was the best.'

3
KNEE DEEP

Of course, we were now hooked on cruising, and the *Candy* was beautiful. As for the staff, they were wonderful, indulging Mum so that when she complained the sun was in her eyes (and the sun wasn't even shining) they pulled the curtains closed. Every meal had to be slightly modified; it was never quite right for her. For instance, she didn't eat any vegetables but cauliflower (without cheese sauce) and peas sometimes. They managed to satisfy her there too, with grace and humour.

The cabins we had on our first cruise were not ideal, so for our second cruise, Peter looked at a ship plan and decided we would take a different double cabin. He rang Trekkers requesting it. The new cabin booked, Peter asked if there were any good single cabins with walk-in showers for Mum.

'Yes, there's one right next to yours,' he replied, then there was a pause and he continued, 'Perhaps you don't want your mother next to you.' They both laughed, but Peter decided to book it anyway.

'You do know we will be summoned whenever Mum wants a button done up or undone, don't you?' I said. 'Still, we will be able to keep an eye on her.'

4

IN OVER OUR HEADS

I couldn't understand why Mum was wearing trousers. She never wore trousers. Always a skirt (she looked a little like Margaret Thatcher, did you ever see Mrs T wearing trousers?) We were travelling across the North Sea en route for the Norwegian fjords when she said, 'I want you to look at my leg.' Please and thank you didn't figure much with my mother-in-law.

I looked at the offending article and didn't like what I saw. 'How long has it been like that?'

'Oh,' she squirmed a bit, 'a day or two now.' She was looking evasive, and I didn't believe her. I felt sure it had been troubling her for several days, if not a week or more.

'Why haven't you been to the doctor about it? You must go to the doctor when surgery opens. Show him and tell him how long it's been like that.'

'Yes,' she agreed, and miracle of miracles, she went. Next thing, we have a telephone call from the ship's doctor. Would we please go down and see him?

Half in and half out of our formal dinner clothing (towelling flip flops go so well with a tuxedo, and are especially in their element on stairs with a long evening dress normally to be worn with heels) we dashed down to him, wondering what on earth he was going to say and whether we would get into trouble for bringing her on the cruise, or she would get into trouble for ignoring the leg. And what exactly was the problem with the leg anyway?

'I think Lilian has DVT,' he stated. 'The leg doesn't look very good at all. I have arranged for you all to go to a clinic in Bergen. A car will pick you up at 9 am tomorrow, and the driver will accompany you to the clinic and stay with you, acting as an interpreter if necessary. I have already emailed the clinic, so you will be expected. The driver will know where to go. The two of you,' indicating Peter and me, 'should be back by lunch.'

'And my mother?' enquired Peter. The doctor put on a doctorish look that eloquently said 'I am not going to be drawn any further', and shrugged his shoulders, 'It's up to the hospital' was all he offered.

At dinner Mum had a captive audience. The whole

table was sympathetic and wished her well. We said little, not wishing to exacerbate the situation or to seem disloyal, but we were both increasingly frustrated by her.

We didn't sleep much that night, and went into breakfast wondering what the day had in store. At a few minutes to nine, reception asked for us, and we went off to the car. The driver's English was impeccable and he explained that we were going to a clinic where Mum would be examined.

The clinic was beautiful and comfortable, and practical chairs were arranged around the room, with pot plants, a coffee-making facility and magazines. We were the only people there, so Mum was sent for straight away.

'Can I see your passport please?' asked an administrator.

'No one told me I needed a passport,' Mum replied.

'Don't worry,' said the administrator reassuringly. 'It probably doesn't matter.'

Mum was taken off for her examination. I waited impatiently, while Peter paced a bit and the driver looked at us sympathetically.

After about ten minutes, Mum returned, smirking. 'I've got to go to hospital for a scan,' she declared. She had always loved hospitals and had a (self-inflicted) operation on an annual basis.

The driver had a quick conversation in Norwegian, then returned to us. 'They are phoning through, so we will be met at the hospital,' he said. 'But I can't come in, so you will have to contact me again when you have finished and I will pick you up.'

A quick drive later and we were at Bergen Hospital, which was deliberately built so that the wards were on the side away from the town and roads, for patients to be peaceful. All the administration faced the road. We were met at reception and given directions to the appropriate department.

'You go along the corridor, take the second left, the first right, go up in the lift to the third floor, turn left, go along that corridor, turn left again... tell you what, I'll take you.' Just as well, as many of the corridors were only accessed by keypads and we didn't have the codes.

Once again, we were met. Peter and I waited in the corridor and Mum was taken into the clinic. It was strange; after the mayhem which is the National Health Service, Bergen Hospital was totally quiet and we saw no one else at all. The place was spotless and beautifully maintained, no scuffs at all and oh, so peaceful.

We sat back, closed our eyes and wondered what the rest of the cruise would have in store for us. Was Mum going to stay in hospital? Would the three of us make it back to the ship before it sailed? Were we all going home now? What... what... what...

Twenty minutes or so later Mum reappeared sporting an enormous bandage from her ankle to her hip and very pleased with the diagnosis; not DVT, but a possible problem with her knee which may have caused the swelling and bruising and a nurse should check it daily. Going downstairs to pay amazed us - it cost the equivalent of £11.

In no time we were back at the ship all ready for lunch. No trousers for Mum now; the bandage was her sole topic of conversation for the rest of the cruise, to our increasing embarrassment. As was 'my nurse', to whom she frequently referred with great pride.

Arriving home, we phoned Peter's brother Geoff as usual, to let him know we were back safely. We told him about the leg.

'Whaaaaaat!' he exclaimed, 'I went to see Mum about a week before you went away and she showed it to me. I told her she had to go to the doctor's before the cruise. She promised me she would. Just wait until I see her next.'

5

ROLL CALL

We didn't always cruise with Mum. We discovered Beeline Cruise Lines, and of course, Mum would only cruise on the *Candy*. We chose a cruise to Canada, which is also, of course, outside Europe (even if you include all the places Mum didn't). The excursion on this particular day was 'The Best of Saguenay'. The coach was like those we had when we went swimming with the school in the 1950s, but instead of smelling of Jeyes fluid, it had a very strong chemical air freshener.

We chose our seats and were a little disconcerted that we had eight sick bags for our convenience, hanging on a hook. Looking round, so did everyone else. We wondered just what the roads must be like and what sort of experiences recent passengers had had.

After an uneventful ride, by which I mean no one was actually sick, we left the coach for our tour around a soap museum and factory. Oh, what soap! It cured everything. We didn't buy any as we prefer unperfumed soap ourselves, and we didn't buy any for anyone else as it sounds a bit tactless to say 'We got you some soap to cure your haemorrhoids / fungus / awful skin condition / whatever', but we enjoyed ourselves and the smell was good after the coach. Back on the coach to a photo stop, off again and on again. It was a bit like the hokey cokey.

No one had thought to count us at any of these places. We climbed back on the coach for the third time and still were not counted, but the coach set off anyway for the next stop; a pulp factory. Off again and on again (still not counted) and we were about to return to the ship, but according to one passenger, there was someone missing. After a few minutes, she arrived, full of apologies, so the coach started off down the drive, but then there was a shout from the back that someone else was missing because there was an unclaimed jacket on an empty seat. So we were counted at last, and yes, you've got it, we were still one person short.

The coach stopped, the guides got off and looked for this person (gender unknown, as it was a unisex jacket) all around the outside of the pulp factory and in the grounds, whilst we waited on the coach for half an hour. Someone did suggest a roll call, but the local guide said she had no list, and our tickets, which had our names on them, had been left at the ship.

We waited. It was clear to us all that no one was around. The pulp mill was closed now for the day and no one was outside in the grounds. We waited again. Then the idea they might have been left at the last photo stop occurred to someone. So we went back there (one and a half hours after the first visit). Well, no one was there, of course. They phoned the ship and got a list of people on the bus (this took time while we waited) which was read over the phone to the Beeline guide on the coach (the local guide had, by now, gone home). The guide was Romanian, with a thick accent, and the person on the other end of the phone had a Spanish accent. Some of the passengers were deaf or chatting, so here the fun really began.

The guide had to read out the names and we had to respond to them, just like at school, and some of us acted just like children too; they should have been sent to the naughty step, although on this old coach, there were only about four steps at the front and they could have all been filled. The guide in her heavy Romanian accent read out:

'Worzel Gummidge.' No, surely not. The coach grew quieter, the disinterested became interested; just the engine, a voice or two and a sweet wrapper made the only noises. She repeated 'Worzel Gummidge', more forcefully and with more confidence this time. There was a little disturbance between a couple who were a row or two in front of us, a short chat, and the lady nodded. The man spoke up.

'I'm Walter Guttridge. Do you mean me?' he asked. He had clearly never been addressed thus before (and why should he have been?) 'Yes, yes, now the next name is Eee... iii... eee Eeyore Will...'

First Worzel Gummidge, now Winnie the Pooh. Well, we had to hand it to her, she knew her English literature!

'I think you mean me,' came a Welsh voice from behind us, 'I'm Ieuan Williams, it's pronounced Yiyun.' He'd said that before, probably many times; it came out with slight resignation and frustration. Why is it that the Welsh language is like Countdown, no vowels for ages, then they all come along at once?

I was now hoping we wouldn't have any Niamhs, Padraigs or Cholmondelys and that we would get back to the boat some time before Christmas (it was September), but she struggled on, fighting a growing amount of laughter and sarcastic remarks from those who had nothing to lose as their names (or something vaguely like them) had already been read out. Some names resembled nothing we could recognise, some sounded the same (she managed to make Terry Watkins sound exactly like Mary Lawless, for example). Then some people had their own name, e.g. Peter and me, as Peter Scott and Rosalind Scott, and other families shared, depending on how the tour was booked, so there were three Ivan Medways. Some people answered to wrong names, so when she called out Peter Scott (which was as clear as a bell) the girl in front of us answered, but her name was Freda Dodd and she complained later, when the guide read out Freda Dodd, that she had already been called. You get the picture?

What with the ayes, whats, sorries and pardons, this went on for a long and lively time and people got surprisingly upset at sharing their names. Ivor Bloodeye really lived up to his name when he got off. Ivan Medway wasn't too pleased either. She referred to him as 'Ivor Headache' the first time, which got everyone tittering, then the second time he was Ivor Headway. It didn't help that she called his name four times and there were only three of them, but after a slight pause a little voice from the back said 'I think you mean me, I'm Irene Treadaway.'

We were about three quarters of the way down the list by this time, and then there was another voice from the back. 'Excuse me, did you know some of us are going out on another trip tonight and are supposed to be having early dinner?'

The guide pulled a face. She clearly did not know, and an early dinner was looking less and less likely. In fact, breakfast wasn't looking too good at the moment, either. Eventually, the roll call ended and we came back to the ship without anyone owning up to the name Shirley Cotton, while Ferda Grunknuckle, Muddy Woodlark and Gobbit Struddle are still a mystery. However, rumour has it that Neil Down and Lettuce Pray, formerly of different parts of the coach, got out together with their arms round each other, to be seen later that night at a table for two in a dark corner of the dining room. A pity really as they were supposed to go to the show in town, modestly called 'La Fabuleuse', but what's in a name?

We got back very, very late, and for some people going out later, it was a bit of a scramble. They were not happy. To cap it all, when we eventually did arrive back at the ship, we were told our absentee had already arrived before us. Over an hour before us in fact. Did she get on the wrong coach? If so, they could not have been counting either.

6

PACK UP YOUR TROUBLES

We booked the middle part of a round the world cruise, Acapulco to Dubai. This meant we had to fly and that meant not much baggage, so we went to Southampton before the *Beeline Beauty* sailed, to put some of our luggage on the ship unaccompanied for the start and end of the voyage. In that way, the cases would be in our cabin for our arrival, and we would have enough clothing for the two and a half months aboard. This is an invaluable service that most cruise lines offer.

We dropped off the luggage, but as the check-in desk was changed at the last minute, there was some confusion. We noticed a couple who were not faring very well. They were in their nineties if they were a day, and they had at least ten cases, all beautifully presented. They all matched and were strapped and labelled with their names, and they carefully put all of them onto three trolleys. He took two trolleys, and she had one. Well, the trolleys had clearly met in a previous life and had serious history. Whichever way one went, the others went in as diametrically different directions as they could. The lady also had a pull-along trolley of her own with a mind of its own. The luggage didn't help either, as the cases were not quite cuboid, being curved. Attractive to look at, but a beast to control, as the cases slid over each other and were completely unstable. They swayed at an alarming rate and speed and everyone else was giving this poor old couple the widest berth possible. Basically, an octopus would have had a hard time controlling their cases, but with only four arms between them, these two had no hope. We lent them our four arms and slightly better progress was made.

A kindly official must have been watching us on CCTV, and was either worried the poor old couple would have coronaries before they checked in, or that there might be a fatal accident with a passenger mown down by hostile luggage, as they could hardly see over the pile of cases they were pushing. Just as we passed a little hatch, it opened and a voice said 'Don't bother to go any further, you can check in here.' Relief all round.

We noticed from the luggage labels that they were

in the room next-door-but-one to us. We told them we would see them in Acapulco, and we confidently expected to help them with their unpacking, which we were sure they would not have had time to complete. After all, it was only three weeks away.

7

ALARM AND EXCURSION

It was a fly cruise. The flight time was very early in the morning, so we booked into a small, independent hotel which would cater for our needs with a serve-yourself continental breakfast close to the airport. It was winter. We arrived in the evening and had a delicious meal. Even Mum was happy with what had been served, and she was excited about the holiday. We decided on a slightly earlier night. Mum's room was opposite ours. Peter set her alarm for 5 am and we said our goodnights.

Peter and I were still reading in bed when the fire alarm rang, for just a second. At 12.30 am, it rang for a second time, also for just a second or so. Peter was fast asleep, I was drowsing in that half-asleep, half-awake kind of way. I muttered to Peter, 'There's something wrong with the alarm,' turned over and slept.

At 2.30 am, there it was again, and this time it went on... and on... and on. Not believing there was a fire, we waited, but it still rang. We dressed quickly, and Peter went across to Mum and told her we had to get up. She was sitting up in bed, listening. We all grabbed warm coats and collected with the other guests on the car park, a shingled area with a few lamp posts; we gathered under one. Mum was wearing her night clothes under a coat. She had no hat as she hated hats (her uniform in the war), no gloves and her footwear was a pair of those fold-up slippers you buy for holidays. They come in a clear pack and look like ballet shoes with elasticated sides; the pack seals with a popper. They are not designed for wearing on frosty, sharp shingle in the middle of the night. Mum was quite tiny and her internal thermostat was not what it had been, so she felt the cold at the best of times.

The fire alarm was still ringing while we guests stood there, looking at the hotel entrance like a tramp convention looking for a bed for the night. It was a strange group. Some had made an attempt at dressing, some hadn't. Some had thought to put on outdoor shoes (or they had forgotten to pack slippers), some were businessmen, and not expecting to need coats so were wearing suit jackets. Some had dragged the duvet with them. No one looked particularly alert. We looked questioning, cold, puzzled and bleary, even in the bitter cold of a frosty night. I wondered about Mum's feet.

'Are you all right?' I asked.

'I'm fine,' she replied, surprisingly chipper, 'Where's the fire?'

'No idea,' I answered,' I can't see any smoke anywhere.'

We stood around hugging ourselves for warmth and eventually, the manager arrived and said a word or two.

'There appears to be something wrong with the fire alarm,' he told us. 'There is no fire, but we can't switch off the alarm. The fire service will be here soon, they will inspect and after that, we can all go back inside.'

'Can't my mother go and wait in the foyer?' asked Peter, 'She's over eighty and freezing.'

'No, sorry, you all have to stay here,' he replied.

'I'm fine,' said Mum.

We continued to wait. It grew no warmer, the shingle grew less comfortable, Mum fidgeted. After three quarters of an hour, the fire engine arrived subtly, slowly and with no fuss. Parked at the other end of the car park and out of our way, the firemen emerged, had a quick confab with the manager and accompanied him inside the hotel. We continued to wait. After a quarter of an hour they reappeared, the hotel was cleared, and we could go back. Mum, unaccountably, had said little, and complained of nothing. We arrived outside our rooms.

'Can you find my alarm clock for me?' asked Mum,
'Isn't it on your bedside table?' said Peter.
'No.'

Peter and I looked at each other, puzzled. What had she done with it? We went into her room. It wasn't on the bedside table; she was right there.

'I thought the ringing was the alarm clock, and I couldn't switch it off,' she explained. 'In the end I threw it across the room. I don't know where it is now.' We searched the room; it couldn't have gone far. Eventually I spotted it, under a chair. It was still ticking and it still told the right time. Peter made sure the alarm was set, and we went out.

'Goodnight Mum,' we said.

'Goodnight. Wasn't that exciting? Just wait till I tell my friends,' she positively gloated.

The alarm clock still worked, but we bought her a radio-controlled clock for holidays and that one was relegated to the smaller spare room in her house where it continued to work accurately until after Mum died.

8
TRAVELLING BUD LITE

The passengers from Gatwick all looked shell-shocked. We had come from Birmingham at about the same time and checked in on the ship. We had seen a scuffle or two, but thought perhaps someone was ill. How wrong can you be?

At dinner the first evening aboard a Mediterranean cruise, Peter and I were at a table for six with our backs to a long table for about 14. We were chatting when we suddenly noticed fixed expressions coming over the faces of our dining companions as they looked through us and at something behind us. We stopped talking.

'Whatever you do,' said Kathy opposite, 'don't look round. It's the travellers.'

'Oh, God, no,' Melanie next to her groaned. Geoff, her husband, looked in concern.

'Don't worry, Mel, they'll be seen to.'

Our faces must have shown that we had no idea what was going on. Dave, Kathy's husband, said, 'You couldn't have been on the Gatwick flight.' We shook our heads. He continued, 'There's a family of travellers here. They were uncontrollable on the flight, and as soon as we landed, despite being told to stay put, they climbed all over the seats to the exit, pushed the people there, including the stewardesses, out of the way and climbed out first. Then, when we were checking in, they pushed in again to get checked in first. Someone said they had won the lottery and were spending it on a cruise for all the family.'

There was some noise from behind us, but we resisted the urge to turn round.

'Oh, what does she look like?' exclaimed Mel.

I looked enquiringly at her. I wanted to know what she looked like, whoever she was.

'Don't look round, she's wearing a bin bag.' Oh, I so wanted to turn round!

'Look at that waiter,' said Geoff. I could see the waiter out of the corner of my eye. It was Den, the waiter we had had on our last cruise on the same ship. Den was from Transylvania and was almost seven feet tall. His twin brother worked in the kitchens.

'Someone's come in with some beer.' Geoff looked suitably appalled. No drink was allowed into the restaurant unless bought with the meal.

'Now they're clearing the plates away,' Geoff continued. He looked completely flummoxed, since they hadn't eaten anything yet. Throughout the meal we were given a running commentary of what was happening on the table for 14 behind us. The travellers comprised two families of two sisters, their husbands and their children making up the fourteen. They insisted on drinking beer at the meal and did not want crockery or cutlery. They didn't want the set meal either; they wanted a hamburger each, plates of chips each and tomato sauce. Den hovered close by at all times, but allowed their requests. The table was cleared and they ate off the tablecloth, eating the hamburger with chips stuck inside the bun, covered and dripping with tomato sauce, drinking the beer out of cans. Their clothing had to be seen to be believed, according to our peeping toms, but of course, we couldn't see and had been put off turning round, expecting a 'what are you looking at?' kind of response.

After feasting on hamburgers and chips, they all got up and trooped out. Bedlam broke out as their activities, spoken about before in hushed tones no doubt, became the topic of the night everywhere.

At the end of the meal, the travellers were to be found in the bar. They were alone; it stayed that way. The rest of the passengers gave them a wide berth. We learned that they could not read, so there were problems when they arrived completing various forms. We also learned that they were confused by the number of noughts on their lire notes for Italy. Stories abounded. They were lost in Rome, someone had stolen their money, they were in a fight in Venice, they had to be picked up from a police station by a taxi, and so the tales grew. All we knew was that in the dining room, Den was never away from their table, where they feasted on the same fare every evening. We had a running commentary on their outfits.

We did see one of them once. One of the daughters fancied herself as Baby Spice. She was young, and that is where the similarity to Baby Spice ended. This young lady was buxom to say the least, reasonably tall and with dark hair which refused point blank to do anything she ever told it. She walked with a sailor's rolling gait and her make-up was Goth, very, very Goth. Wild was not the word; she looked alien. She arrived in the dining hall (we arrived behind her) wearing a tiny pink skirt, white briefs (the sort that were not meant to be seen, but were) underneath, and a top with spaghetti straps. On her feet were tennis shoes with socks with frills. So far, so good, except the briefs – Baby Spice would have looked good in almost such an outfit. However, our buxom miss was also wearing a sports bra (white) under the top (black). You could see more sports bra that you could of the top and skirt together.

When they arrived in the dining room, there was a lull in the conversation, and we could see the eyes turning in her (our) direction. She looked around, sniffed, put her hands under her extremely large boobs and gave them a big boost. The boobs rose, so we were told (why were we never at the ringside, always at the back?) but the top covering them did not; it had got caught under the bra. A sight for sore eyes.

Later, the bin bag returned with a pair of shoes to match. She had made a sort of sole and cut strips of bin bag to cross thread all the way up her legs, Roman style.

Every evening they commandeered the bar, and every evening the rest of the passengers kept away. Towards the end of the cruise, it was the wedding anniversary of one of the couples. The entire family arrived in all their splendour – the men even wore ties! Skirts were long, the paste jewellery came out in piles. They appeared almost normal. The cake arrived with a candle and the loving couple sat staring into each other's eyes and then blew out the candle, the cake was shared and they left, we all sighed, *ahhhhhhh!*

On the last day, one cabin was opened up for passengers leaving on late flights to deposit their luggage for the day. Gatwick was going last, Birmingham next to last. We went down to offload the luggage, but were turned away at the door. It stank of booze and cigarettes and another passenger said, 'I'm going to complain, the travellers are all in there, in the beds, smoking and drinking and I for one, am not leaving my luggage there.' there was general agreement that it wouldn't do. A complaint was made and we were allowed another cabin. The travellers' drinks bill came to nearly a thousand pounds in the one-week cruise.

We met Den again the following year, and he told us that the company had had to fumigate the room, but then, because of all the cigarette burns in the carpet, it had to be stripped out and completely refurbished. People going back on the Gatwick flight were apprehensive, frightened even, but we never did find out if anything happened as we have never met any of those passengers again.

9

A TIMELY TUMBLE

We had just boarded the ship with Mum and were unpacking in our cabin when the phone rang. It was Mum, from her cabin.

'I've fallen over and can't get up, you'll have to come and help me.'

Peter had taken the call. 'It's Mum, she's fallen over. Luckily, she was near the phone. Come on, let's see what she's done.'

We left everything and dashed to her cabin as quickly as possible. The door was ajar, which was also lucky, as otherwise we would have had to find the cabin steward. Rushing in, we found Mum sitting smirking on the floor with her legs straight out in front of her. Looking round at the cabin, we noticed that a two-seater sofa had been placed against a wall, about fifty centimetres behind a coffee table, with a lamp table placed beside the sofa to one side. The telephone was on the lamp table and Mum was sitting on the floor between the sofa and the coffee table, legs stretched out, under the table. The telephone was still within reach on the lamp table.

We moved the coffee table out and picked Mum up, advising her to sit on the sofa for a minute or two. 'How did you manage to fall down there?' asked Peter. Mum ignored him, so I asked the same question and she ignored me too. Peter and I exchanged a look. We didn't think for a second that she had fallen, she couldn't have. It just wasn't possible.

'Are you all right? Have you hurt yourself?' asked Peter.

Mum looked round. 'No, I'm fine.'

'Well,' he continued, 'if you fall over before we have even left Southampton, what on earth are you going to do after we leave? Perhaps we shouldn't have come.'

We made sure all was well and departed for our cabin. 'She did that deliberately,' I said. 'She just wanted to know how quickly the cavalry would come if she really did fall over.'

Peter nodded his agreement. Just to make sure, I tried to fall in the same place in our cabin - I couldn't; the best I could do was what we assumed Mum had done. I stood between the sofa and the coffee table in our cabin, then sat on the sofa and slid down the front of it until I was sitting on the floor, feet out in front under the table. I just fitted, although my knees grazed the table.

Mum was never one to bear anything in silence, but we didn't refer to her fall again, and neither did she, nor did she complain of any bruises or knocks.

10

AND THE BAGGAGE WENT ROUND AND ROUND

'Would Mr and Mrs Scott of cabin 207 come to reception as soon as possible please?'

We had just boarded and unpacked and were now having a drink in the Café de Paris. What on earth had we done? We gulped the drinks and went downstairs to reception as soon as we could, i.e. instantly. There were a couple of elderly women waiting, but they indicated for us to go first.

'We're Mr and Mrs Scott,' Peter introduced us.

'Ah, good,' said the receptionist, 'Do you have all your luggage?'

'Yes thank you, in fact we have just unpacked.'

'Are you sure it was your luggage?'

'Well, yes.' Peter was a bit flummoxed. We were usually able to identify our luggage because, well, we recognized what we had packed, we hadn't done it long ago, and our memories were reasonable.

'Only this lady here,' she indicated the smaller of the ladies – much smaller, the other lady was about four times her size – 'picked up the wrong bag in Cyprus when we boarded and she has a bag marked Scott instead. Are you sure it isn't yours?'

We were quite sure, but sympathized with the lady who hadn't any of her own luggage. 'It's exactly the same case as I've got, I didn't think to check the label,' she said. 'Stupid, now I look back.'

'It's an easy mistake to make when you are under pressure,' I agreed, and commiserated also with Mr Scott, who, presumably, was left at the airport looking at a bag strikingly like his but with another name on it going round on the carousel.

'What happens now?' I asked. I felt for the lady with only the clothes she stood up in.

'We send this bag back at the next port and hope that the airport has sent on this lady's and we can pick it up then,' the receptionist said. The next port was Rhodes; not far.

'I'll see what I can buy in the shop,' said the little lady.

'Oh, never mind,' responded her companion mildly,

'you can wear my knickers, Edie.'

'Up to my armpits, Mavis.' Edie began to giggle... so did Mavis... so did Peter... so did I, and eventually so did the normally po-faced receptionist.

We saw them in Rhodes. They were about ten metres away, wandering up the main street; we waved.

'I'm wearing my own knickers!' called Edie to us excitedly, and very loudly, oblivious to the fact that the whole world understands English. The people around immediately stopped and stared. 'I had my case back this morning, thank God.' We all had a good giggle again as the horrified locals looked on.

11

CONTRABAND

Events around the world had changed the rules on flying. Post 9/11, cruise lines had changed their rules too, to keep in line. We were off with Mum on a fly cruise on the *Candy*. Mum didn't always read the paperwork she was sent, so we went over it with her.

'You can only take one piece of cabin baggage with you on the plane,' we advised her, 'and it has to be really small.' We gave her the dimensions, comparing them with a box she had which was about the same size. 'You have to leave anything that can be used as a weapon at home, too; scissors, knives or nail files. You can't take any of them.'

'Yes, yes,' she said, waving it all away.

The car we ordered picked us up and drove us over to Mum. The driver took her case, and put it in the boot. Mum was ready to climb into the car. She was holding two handbags.

'Why have you got two handbags? You can't take two with you on the plane,' I said. I was irritated; it would have been so easy for her to pack all her bits in her case, which was clearly not full.

'One's my handbag, the other's my holiday bag. I always take them both.' Mum was quite adamant.

'We read the rules to you, they have changed, and you can't take two bags.' Oh, she was so annoying. 'When we arrive, you'll have to pack one of the bags in your suitcase, and don't argue.' Peter was holding the door for her. 'Now get in.' Mum got in.

At the airport she refused to pack her bag, saying they wouldn't mind, so we checked in.

'Did you pack this yourself, has it been out of your sight?' the assistant said. 'What are you carrying on with you?'

Mum lifted her bags.

'Only one bag allowed, you'll have to pack one in your suitcase.'

Peter and I looked at each other. YESSSSS! Someone to support us.

We packed one bag into the case in silence. It took ages as Mum swapped things over from one bag to the other and then back again. The airport was busy, and we thrashed about in front of the check-in and got in everyone's way. Eventually, we were all checked in and off went the suitcases.

We went to security, belts off, shoes off, watches off and through the metal detector. Mum's bag went through the contraband detector first. She was stopped by an official, who opened her handbag. He found a pair of manicure scissors, a nail file, a fruit knife and then another pair of manicure scissors. Lastly, he found a small penknife. He collected them together and handed back the handbag.

'You can take it now, but these are confiscated,' he said.

'I didn't know I couldn't take them, no one told me,' said Mum.

12

WATER MUSIC

My family is fairly musical. My mother went to the Royal Academy to study piano and voice, I had a cousin in the BBC Concert Orchestra and our niece sings with the Royal Liverpool Philharmonic Choir. Music was my second subject at college and I can hold a tune when I sing, so, having just joined the ship, I thought I would join the ship choir.

I went along to the venue, where about thirty men were singing a fine rendition of 'Old MacDonald's Farm'. Surprised there were no women, I asked if it was the choir. The reply was that it was the real choir, but the other choir was 'over there', where a few staid, suntanned women were sitting in silence like a row of ducks. In front of them was an electric organ on an X-stand. I smiled and joined them; I was ignored.

A few more ladies of a paler complexion who had just boarded then arrived, asking if they were in the right place. They were altogether friendlier. The leader arrived and he gave a quarter of an hour's talk on how good the choir had been in the last sector where they had performed 'Iolanthe'. I couldn't imagine doing an operetta in three weeks, an hour a day only on sea days. The pale faces became paler, with a 'what have I let myself in for?' expression.

We were then asked to get to know each other. Bedlam ensued, during which the X-stand under the organ collapsed. There was a massive crash and then complete silence. The organ had fallen apart. Strong men set it up again, but it wouldn't work. Plugs were fiddled with, the organ was kicked, bits were blown on and through, but the only results were squeaks and shrieks from the protesting instrument.

Five minutes later, a member of the crew was called; when he arrived he was not told of the accident, just that the organ wouldn't work. Despite this total lack of information, in ten seconds he had twiddled a few things and lo and behold, the organ worked. Magic! It was more interesting watching him than the rehearsal. I was regretting not joining the 'Old MacDonald' choir as I thought I probably had more in common with them.

We were told how to read music. If the dots go up, so do you – now you can read music. We were told about harmonizing. If it sounds good, you are good, if it doesn't, you aren't. We learned how to breathe (thank goodness for that, how had I survived until now?) and how to sing a high note - open your mouth wide. I wasn't keen on the choice of music and during my time on the cruise the choir gave one or two concerts, but without me, I didn't go again.

After we left the ship, with three weeks of the cruise still to go, I heard the choir was doing 'Bugsy Malone' on the last leg (or maybe on their last legs). Now correct me if I am wrong, but wasn't it written for children? I just can't see the effect of bald heads and paunches together with varicose veins, fat waists and dangly boobs having quite the same impact.

13

FINDING THE LIFEBOAT

Irritating Imogen joined us on a cruise around the UK (Mum's Europe had extended while she was travelling with us). Well, irritating Imogen didn't actually travel with us, but she was assigned the same dinner table for eight and was in the cabin on the other side of Peter and me from Mum. We first met her for lifeboat drill. She was in the corridor as we emerged from our cabin, a tiny, beautifully-dressed and coiffed elderly lady with white hair, a quivering lower lip and wide, innocent pale blue eyes that looked as though they were just about to spill tears.

'I don't know what to do or where to go,' she

murmured querulously as she left her cabin, life jacket in hand.

'That's okay,' we said, assuming that this must be her first cruise on the *Candy*, or possibly her first cruise on any ship, for you learn very quickly about lifeboat drill, even if you learn nothing else. 'You will be at our muster station and in our lifeboat, come with us.'

Mum appeared from her cabin at this point and we explained that 'this lady' wasn't sure what to do and would accompany us to drill. Mum did not look too thrilled to be sharing us. She pinched her lips, stomped a bit and said nothing all the way to the muster station. The three of us put on our life jackets, Peter adjusting the strap that went round Mum's chest, and kept the life jacket in place for Mum.

We sat down. I looked round and there was irritating Imogen standing there, life jacket in hand, doing nothing.

'Let me help you,' I offered, and as she stood there, arms out like a young child waiting to be dressed, I put on her jacket.

'Oh, thank you so much,' she whispered, 'I'm not used to all this.'

'Don't worry,' I replied, 'we have cruised a lot, stick with us and you can't go wrong.'

'Oh, thank you,' she whispered again, 'Is that your mother?'

'No, my mother-in-law,' I said, and made the introductions.

Irritating Imogen followed us back to the cabin, and I took off her jacket.

'You have been so helpful, are you going on the excursion this evening?' she asked.

'Yes, do you want to stay with us?'

'Oh, can I? Your mother-in-law is so lucky, my family wouldn't come with me, but we are going to speak each day on the phone.'

We agreed to meet in the lounge for the trip the next day. We travelled together. Irritating Imogen sat next to Mum on the coach, where Mum completely ignored her all the way there and all the way back. Peter and I agreed it was a shame Imogen (we hadn't assigned her the title 'irritating' at that point) had come on her first cruise all alone, particularly as she was 88, a point she had made to us during the excursion. She was just a year older than Mum. We thought she was very brave.

The following evening she attached herself to us as we were going down to dinner, telling us she didn't yet know how to get to the dining room. Peter and I sat protectively, each side of Mum. She had difficulty in making general conversation, preferring to talk to one of us exclusively. Irritating Imogen was the other side of me.

'You may have noticed I have my own teabags,' Imogen whispered. I hadn't. 'I love these,' she continued, showing me a Lady Grey teabag. 'You can't get them in England. I had them once and wanted to know where to buy them, so I telephoned the company and they said they didn't distribute them in England, but that I was so polite to them on the phone, they would send some to me as an exception, and they did.'

'How kind of them.' I volunteered. I vaguely recognised Lady Grey; maybe I was mixing her up with Earl Grey.

The waiters on Trekkers only have to see you once to remember you, and I was pleased that they were able to recognise Irritating Imogen quickly, as were the wine waiters, the maître d'hôtel and other crew who came into contact with her; I thought it was kind and would make her feel more at home on an unknown ship. She carried on chatting.

'When I had my children, the firm I worked for told me they would keep my job open for as long as I liked, as I was the best person they had ever employed,' she continued. I felt Mum pinching my arm on the other side.

'Where did you buy your dress?' she asked.

'You were with me when I bought it, in Chichester.' Mum was not liking me talking to Imogen.

'How many dresses did you bring with you?' Mum was competing now.

'I told you yesterday when you asked; five,' I answered testily, but Mum couldn't take a hint. I suspected Imogen was enjoying it too, as she interrupted when Mum was asking questions as Mum interrupted when Imogen spoke. It was a long dinner.

We decided not to sit each side of Mum in future, as then at least one of us could have a conversation with someone else. Meanwhile, Peter, like me, had noticed that most of the dining staff knew Irritating Imogen, and the following morning, the security officer called out to her as we were off on an excursion.

'Hi, Imogen,' he called, 'what sort of mischief are you getting into now?'

We were beginning to wonder if it really was her first cruise.

A few days later, Irritating Imogen invited the three of us into her cabin for 6 pm to help her drink a bottle of champagne. When we arrived at her cabin she answered the door, saying 'what a surprise, what are you doing here?' No champagne then, perhaps Imogen had a bad memory. Mum was delighted; she hadn't wanted to come and Peter had insisted that we all accept her kind invitation.

At dinner, Irritating Imogen was sitting beside me again.

'Did you notice my cat brooch I was wearing yesterday?' she asked.

'No, sorry.' I hadn't.

'It matches some earrings and is worth a lot of money. I think someone has stolen it.'

'Surely not?' I shook my head in mystification.

'I was on my own today, and I reported my burglary and some of the crew spent all morning in my cabin looking for it.' She sounded quite triumphant.

'Did they find it?'

'Oh no!' She still sounded triumphant.

I was beginning to wonder about Imogen. I was just a trifle suspicious. She seemed to turn up whenever we left the cabin, always wondering if we could help her over something quite trivial. Between Irritating Imogen and Mum (quite literally) we began to dread stepping outside. It was also becoming clear that Mum hated her, and Imogen knew it, and enjoyed it, asking us more and more often for favours, always thanking us profusely in her trademark whisper. Later she would tell Mum how wonderful we were and how lucky she was. Mum would purse her lips, raise her eyebrows and look away, saying nothing.

A couple of days later, Irritating Imogen sat next to me at dinner again.

'Do you know what I do when I am at a loose end?' she asked.

'No,' I said, knowing I was about to hear.

'I walk somewhere on the ship and when I see a member of the crew, I tell them I am lost and can't find my way back to my cabin. Then they take me back, they are very nice to me. My father used to say I was mischievous when I got my brother into trouble. I sometimes pretend to be stupid, but I'm not, am I?'

'You certainly are not,' I said. I thought of the number of times Mum had told us Irritating Imogen was 'putting it on' and the times we had defended her, a poor old lady on her first cruise without her family to help her. I was beginning not to blame the family. She was worse than Mum, and saccharine to boot.

'Exactly how many times have you cruised with Trekkers?' I asked.

'Oh, dozens of times,' she answered brightly. 'I had my 80th birthday on the *Candy*. They like me so much, they gave me a special party.' Well, that answered a few questions.

A day or two later, we were seated on a coach, Mum in front of us, on her own with her bags on the seat next to her to put off singles joining her. When Irritating Imogen climbed aboard, almost last, she walked down the aisle, looking for a seat. She came to Mum.

'Would you like me to sit beside you?' she asked.

Mum didn't even look at her. 'No,' she said.

I mouthed 'sorry' to Imogen as she passed us. Mum didn't need to be so rude; irritating Imogen was never rude. She continued down the aisle and presumably found somewhere. At least, she didn't come back.

A local tour guide came down the coach giving out maps. She came to Mum.

'Would you like a map, madam?'

Mum didn't even look at her. 'No,' she said.

14

SENT TO WALK THE PLANK

We were in the dining room the first evening of our very first cruise without Mum, minding our own business and eating our dinner. There was a bit of a hubbub behind us, but we were talking and didn't turn round. The following day we arrived at our first destination and noticed cases by the gangway off the ship. We didn't think about them again until we were told what the commotion in the dining room had been.

It transpired that a couple at a table for two had had a row. He had thrown the champagne bottle at her and she had thrown the ice bucket at him. They were escorted out of the dining room and were now on their way home, never to be seen again.

15

BECOMING DELUSIONAL

'How far is it to the end of the road?' my mother-in-law asked me one day when we were alone at her house. Peter was doing some chores for her upstairs. I had learned to be very wary of her questions à propos of nothing.

'How far do you think it is?' I hedged.

'About one hundred yards, I should think.'

'I think that's about right. Why did you want to know?'

'My friend's got a disabled badge, so I want one, and my friend said that to get one, you should only be able to walk about fifty yards. So that's about right, I can only walk fifty yards. I can't walk to the end of the road. I've got an application form, and I can't fill it in, so Peter will have to do it.'

I remained silent. She had walked considerably more than a hundred yards round the shops a week or two before. I didn't think she was eligible for a disabled badge, but I wasn't going to interfere.

Peter came downstairs and Mum asked him to complete the form.

'Are you sure you need this?' he asked.

'Yes' she replied, 'you get your parking free.'

Peter and I exchanged a look as he began to complete the form.

'It says "do you use a walking aid". You don't, do you?'

'No.'

'You don't need help in the house or the garden, do you?'

'No' she answered, and so it went on. It was quite clear that Mum needed no help at all, and the 'only being able to walk fifty yards' bit stood out like a sore thumb.

'You need two photos, signed on the back,' I told her.

'I've got those here,' she said, and she produced two photos taken in a photo booth.

'Did you have these done at St Audries Bay?' Peter enquired,

'Yes.'

'Well, they are about thirty years out of date.'

'Too bad, they'll have to lump it, I'm not having any more done.' So Peter took the photos and put them in an envelope ready for posting.

'I'll take them to the box,' I offered. The pillar box was about fifty yards from the house, so Mum was not going to be willing to take it – after all, she could only walk there, she couldn't walk back.

'Oh, I was going to take it after you had gone home, but you can do it if you like,' she said.

'That's okay,' I said, and off I went.

'She'll never get it,' Peter said on the way home, 'She might need it in a year or two, but not now.'

One week later

We were back at Mum's, as the excursion booklet for our next cruise had arrived. We were going round the Baltic. Mum had been before and enjoyed it. She greeted Peter with the usual pile of chores, and after I had put our flowers in water she proudly said, 'I heard from the council about the disabled badge. They phoned the other day, they said there wasn't a problem, and I'd get the badge, but the photo was too old, so I had another one taken and took it to the office myself yesterday.' I was stupefied.

Peter arrived back downstairs and Mum started choosing the excursions. We got to discussing Tallinn.

'Oh, I love Tallinn,' she said.

'Well, there's only the walking tour of Tallinn if you want to go into the town, otherwise it's a coach trip round Estonia.'

'I want to go to Tallinn,' she stated finally and with conviction, brooking no argument from us.

'Well, it says here you must be able to walk one thousand metres over cobbles.'

'Oh, I can do that.'

Peter and I were hit by the gobsmackers again.

16

A BIT OF A HICCUP

On formal nights on various cruise lines, senior crew guest on some of the tables, arriving in full formal uniform. They are easily identified by the stripes on their epaulettes or cuffs – the more stripes, the more senior they are. The stripes are generally gold and white, but for the doctor, they are gold and red. The table usually settles with the passengers first, and the guest arrives last. Anyway, that's what is supposed to happen, but we are dealing with people here, where nothing goes smoothly.

It was the doctor who attended our table on this particular formal night. A couple at the table were late, which was quite usual for them; they would spend the day in the bars until they arrived in a state where they couldn't really tell the time. Meanwhile, in the dining room, time came and went and the doctor arrived, sporting his red stripes, which were pretty easy to spot, carried as they were proudly on his shoulders and completed by the rest of his very smart uniform. His wife was with him, wearing an evening dress to die for. The waiters hung about a bit for the others to arrive, but eventually they couldn't wait any more, and menus were handed out.

Several minutes after introductions had been made, our two late arrivals wove their rather inebriated way between the dining tables, eventually arriving at ours, pulling out their chairs and sitting. This took a moment or two. They missed once or twice, she giggled inanely and he hiccupped, burped softly and murmured to himself 'better out than in' – for him, maybe. No one looked at them, I found my cutlery endlessly fascinating.

Once seated, the lady tried to get her eyes in focus. She obviously thought there was something different about the table, so she squinted a bit, just to make sure. Eventually, she leaned across the table, addressing the doctor directly, her shoulder strap dropping, showing as she did so a great deal of cleavage and rather more on one side than we would wish to see.

'And who the hell are you?' she demanded.

'The doctor,' he replied with a surprised look.

Leaning over to Peter, who was sitting next to her, she said, 'Do you think I am a bit tipsy?'

Well, what could he say?

17

I-SPY

Tallinn is one of the most beautiful northern capitals, and only accessible on foot. We were dropped off at the city gate for our walking tour. Mum had agreed she could walk 1,000 metres over cobbles, but she hated to walk, and a rough surface only made it worse. On this particular day, she insisted on wearing thin-soled, open toed sandals. During the war, her uniform had included lace-up shoes, and at the end of the war she had vowed never to wear lace-ups again. She kept to it.

We both wore trainers; ideal for cobbles, as they had air cushions in the soles, but Mum would not entertain the thought of donning something as dowdy as trainers. At home she always used the car (Mum and driving is a whole new book) and if she had two destinations 100 metres apart, she took the car in between so she had minimal walking. We were dreading this excursion and had already spoken to the cruise escort, Sophie, who was tail-end Charlie for the morning.

We disembarked from the coach. The local guide had already set off, talking as he went about the architecture. Mum proceeded slowly; very soon we were lagging behind.

The problem with Tallinn is that it is a maze of tiny streets, some only twenty or thirty paces long, but the good thing about it is that the architecture is wonderful almost everywhere, so the group in front of us stopped frequently to admire and snap it. For about twenty minutes we kept the group in view. We didn't hear much of the commentary because just as we caught up with them, it finished and the local guide took off again. Mum was getting fed up. 'How can I get any rest if they keep going off as soon as we reach them?' she asked Sophie. She stopped and refused to move on, dramatically huffing and puffing for a few minutes.

Sophie was looking anxious; we were now losing sight of the group round corners. Peter suggested she should go on to the corner to keep the group in view while we tried to get Mum moving at a reasonable rate. Sophie ran off to the corner, stopped and beckoned to us, and we hurried forward, hoping Mum would take the hint; she didn't. She started walking on the spot in tiny steps. She was getting nowhere.

'Mum, come on,' I insisted, 'we are getting left behind.'

'I'm tired,' she wailed, still walking on the spot. Peter and I took both arms and frog-marched her to the end of the road. Sophie was still there, anxiously watching the others.

'Look,' I suggested to her, 'you go on to the corner to keep the group in view, I'll keep you in view at the next corner, and keep Mum and Peter in view behind me, that way we can cover several corners at once.'

Sophie agreed. Before she ran off to the next corner, she explained that the tea stop was at the town hall, so we would know what to ask for if we did get separated. She disappeared round the next bend and I ran up to it, keeping her in view. We must have looked like something out of a James Bond film, one spy watching another, while a hostage was being dragged to who knows where.

Peter pulled Mum along, keeping me in view. Sophie disappeared and I ran down the next little road, looking from side to side down little alleys, in case the group had wandered off down one of them, I stopped and waited for Peter. I thought that if I donned my sunglasses, I would look even more like a spy.

In this halting, hiccupping way, we eventually arrived at the town hall, where Sophie was waiting outside for us. Fortunately, we hadn't been taken for spies and dragged off to the central police station. Perhaps the locals were used to this kind of thing?

'We'll be here for some time,' said Sophie. 'We've got a dance group scheduled after the refreshments, so Lilian can sit down for a bit.'

'If I'd known how fast you were going, I wouldn't have come,' Mum complained as she reached us. Going inside, there were no tables with three seats available to us. My heart sank; we needed to do something before Mum noticed. Fortunately, her first stop had been the loo.

Sophie collected some chairs, presently only used for coats, cameras and handbags, as Peter found a table. By the time Mum appeared, we had a table and four chairs. We also had four cups of coffee and some cakes. Mum sat down just as the dancers started.

'Oh, I've seen this before,' she complained loudly, scraping her chair back as she stretched for a cake.

'Shhhh!' another passenger hushed her. Sophie, Peter and I exchanged looks. Mum looked as though she hadn't heard. We watched the intricate dancing and listened to the music, trying to appreciate it and trying to relax.

As it finished, Peter suggested to Sophie that she should stay with the group and we should make our own way back, using the most direct route, meeting them at the city gate. Reluctantly, she agreed, as we assured her we knew the way and anyway, there was a map of Tallinn inside the hall we were in, and we would refer to it before leaving, just to make sure.

We waited for the rest of the group to leave, then followed, but stayed on the main road when they branched off down a small road.

'Why are we going this way?' asked Mum.

'We are going straight back, so you don't have to walk as far.' Peter was adamant.

'But we were going to a trinket shop on the way back.'

'You can't walk fast enough, we're going straight back to the coach,' from me.

'I want to go to the shop.' Mum stopped. She had her stubborn expression on her face. We knew it well. 'If I go faster, can we go to the shop?'

'You won't go faster.' Me again.

'Yes, I will, I want to go to the shop. Is it this way?' and she trotted off, following the group.

'It's right by the city wall, where we came in. We will go by it whichever way we go,' Peter said as she turned round.

'If I walk fast, we can get there first,' she said. You could see the cogs turning round in her head.

'Well, you'd better get walking then,' I said and started off smartly. She came with me. She kept up all the way back to the wall. No problems at all.

Mum loved the trinket shop. I have no idea if she

bought anything or not; she didn't ask for my advice this time. I think she thought she had pushed us far enough.

18
ADRIFT

It was two in the morning, and I was suddenly awake and alert. Peter was snoring gently beside me. It was unusually dark; normally I could see the light of the corridor round the cabin door frame. It was warm and silent. It was completely silent.

I sat up and waited, listening to the silence. I carefully got out of bed and walked to the window. I looked out; no wash to show we were moving, lights appearing to be stationary way out on the horizon. I went back to bed and switched on the bedside light, but nothing happened, no electricity. What was going on? We were still out in the Atlantic somewhere, miles from land. It didn't feel good, it didn't feel right.

I gently nudged Peter until he woke.

'It's completely silent,' I whispered, 'the engines have stopped, we aren't moving, there's no air conditioning, no electricity. Something's wrong.'

He sat up in bed next to me and we waited, not sure quite what for, but we waited. Half an hour went by,

'I think we ought to get dressed' he said, 'just in case'.

We blundered around in the dark; it was so dark our eyes just hadn't got used to it. We dressed and collected our medication and went to the loo (not flushing it, as we never did between midnight and 7am). We continued to wait.

'Thank goodness Mum isn't with us,' Peter said.

'She'd be well and truly panicking by now,' I replied, thinking it wouldn't take much for me to panic.

We sat on the bed, fully dressed, waiting for the emergency bell to send us to the lifeboats. We were quite sure we had completely broken down for some reason. After an hour and a quarter, the bedside light came on; thank goodness, electricity. About ten minutes later, on came the air conditioning and at last, the engines. We undressed, feeling slightly foolish and climbed back into bed.

The following morning the captain explained that an engine had been switched off for maintenance in the middle of the night, so as not to inconvenience us, and then the other engine had been switched off as the maintenance couldn't be done with it going. All was well now and we would soon make up the lost time. We heard that dozens of people had made their way to reception in various states of dress and undress. Some had been distressed, some had just thought it was all a joke, but all had wanted to know when the engines were going to come on again. Perhaps next time, a little warning the night before that this might happen would be prudent. If it happens again, we will try to ignore it.

19

ALMOST OVERBOARD

Dinner gives a novel perspective on storms at sea. There we sat one evening at our table for two, thinking how relatively peaceful it was and crash, the bottle of wine (it had to be red, didn't it?) on the next table had fallen over, taking out everything in its path, comprising pretty well everything on the table – one wet lady, two wet chairs and a wet carpet. They moved to another table, another crash and a whole cupboard full of crockery opened of its own accord and threw its contents at an unassuming waiter who happened to be in the firing line. Meanwhile, drawers and cupboards all along one side of the dining room opened and shut, throwing out or just dropping contents onto the floor for the waiters to fall over, while we were holding on like grim death to anything stable. It was a long mealtime...but not as spectacular as breakfast...

We were coming back across the Bay of Biscay after the world's first official mystery cruise with Mum, which was booked up within days. Fortunately, we were due to go and see Mum the day after the new brochure came out, so we booked her usual room, although we had to book ours some distance from her. Looking back, it seems amazing that Mum went, as she much preferred going to places she already knew, but the idea of waking up not knowing where she was interested her. Trekkers was promising new ports they had not used before and she liked the probable mixture of old and new places to explore.

When we arrived on the ship, there were several members of the press to greet us, as the idea of a mystery cruise had caught the British imagination. They wanted to interview someone from east London, and Mum volunteered.

'I'm interested to know why you booked this cruise,' the journalist said, 'or are you just mad?'

Mum's mind must have gone blank. She giggled, 'I don't know, I must be mad,' she wailed, and that was the end of the interview. We checked the papers on our return; nothing.

The mystery cruise was a hit; new places (some a bit odd, some a bit smelly) and amazing things to do while at sea (killing each other with bananas was one).

Peter was ill at one point, but more of that later.

So, we were returning across the famed Bay of Biscay and the weather was not good. A hurricane travelling across the Atlantic was due to bump into a storm along the English Channel coming the other way, just as we were entering the Channel. Lovely! We bumped and jumped our way through the waves - a huge long swell, and the poor old *Candy* was doing the best she could. We were in breakfast. Now Trekkers prides itself on its food - in my opinion, the best afloat. Its dining rooms had, in those days, to be seen to be believed.

In the centre of the room was the breakfast bar. In the centre of the breakfast bar was a huge, one-and-a-half-metre-high ice carving, and to each side of this, metre-high floral displays, and fruit displays (not to be touched) just a little smaller. Round them were the big hoppers for cereal, large bowls of already cut fresh fruit, bowls of tinned fruit, bowls of yoghurt, dispensers of fruit juice – a choice of about six – then there were trays of all the components of a full English breakfast, trays of breads, brioche, croissants, Danish pastries, ham and cheese, individual pots of yoghurt, bowls of honey and marmalade and so it went on. A huge table covered in pristine white cloths was covered by delicacy after delicacy, and of course, the crockery on which to put your choices. Mouthwatering just wasn't in it, you would have been forgiven for drooling a small lake. Round this central display were arranged the breakfast tables, all anchored to the floor, at which several hundred people were eating breakfast, some enjoying a relaxing cup of tea or coffee, some chatting to the waiters. A peaceful introduction to the day, or at least, as peaceful as it could be.

Mum was on one side of the table, we were on the other. We could see out of the portholes that the sea covered them one minute and they were clear the next, and somehow Peter had a sixth sense...

Suddenly, the ship tilted 90 degrees towards Peter and me. It seemed as though we all finished up on the ground. It was like standing under the Niagara Falls times ten, completely surrounded by noise, which continued for several seconds that seemed to go on for ever. The chap the other side of me from Peter was covered in scalding coffee. I slightly scalded my foot, while Peter managed to escape anything by grabbing hold of the table, which was the only thing fixed to the floor; he said he could almost see it coming. I got up and helped the chap next to me up. There was no one upright in the entire room, except Mum, sitting there like Boudicca, looking round her as if to say 'now why did you all disappear?' and Peter, still hanging on for grim death to his side of the table. The scene was of utter devastation, as everything on the display was now on the floor, shattered. The waiters looked horrified, upset, almost in tears.

'What's happening about my breakfast?' Mum asked us. We said nothing.

'Is anyone hurt?' asked the maître d' hotel. No one appeared to be badly hurt; there were one or two scalds and a few small bumps and that was it. We had started putting broken crockery back on the tables when we heard the captain say, 'Oh, that was a good one, hope you were okay on the stairs.' Silence, then laughter and a couple of minutes later, 'I gather there was a slight incident in the dining room. I am now going to ask you to go back to your cabins and stay there until further notice, but please be careful on the way, particularly on the stairs. If you have not already had your breakfast, you can have room service.'

'I want my breakfast here,' whined Mum.

'You can have room service in your cabin,' Peter replied,

'I'm not going to my cabin on my own,' she persisted, 'I'm coming to yours.'

'If you do that, we'll have to put a label on your door so the cabin stewardess knows where you are, because they will have to come round and check,' I said.

So she came with us and we ordered room service. We warned her it would be a long time as an awful lot of people would use the service, but in the event, it was only just over half an hour, which we thought was pretty good.

'My friends are going to enjoy this story, but I don't know where I am going to tell them we have been,' she said.

We looked at her. 'What's the problem? Tell them you've been where we have been.'

'I can't do that, we've only been to Spain. I can't tell them I've only been there. I know, I'll tell them we've been to Greece and the Canaries.'

'What on earth's the point of that?' asked Peter. 'Tell them the truth.'

'We've only been gone fourteen days,' I joined in. 'You couldn't possibly do both those places in that time anyway. Tell your friends it was a mystery.'

Sadly, Trekkers does not display its breakfasts with ice carvings, floral displays and displays of fruit any more. That day, everything was cleaned and cleared by lunchtime, and you would have had no idea that anything untoward had happened.

We never did know where Mum told her friends she had been.

20

OUR LIVES IN OUR HANDS

Peter and I enjoyed walking round the promenade deck when on holiday. What we hadn't realised was that we needed dangerous sports insurance in order to do it. Each day we walked round the deck, as four/five/six circuits made a mile (depending on the size of the ship) and we walked the designated way - anticlockwise. The deck itself was always wood planks, well finished and caulked and in itself, not the least bit dangerous. Runners, in order not to cause hazards, had to keep to antisocial hours, something like 0100 to 0600, we were never sure, as we were never around at those times, although we did see runners.

In some places the deck was as wide as a couple of metres, but in others, on some ships, it was narrow, very narrow. We always tried to walk three miles, but that feat was often full of unexpected challenges. The first was shuffleboard and deck quoits, both played on the promenade deck from time to time. These were organised games and attracted lots of competitors, and should have taken precedence over the walkers, so we tried to wait until it was convenient to them and then we dashed between the legs of the players and hoped we wouldn't be taken out at the ankles by someone or something flying around in the game. We would then catch up with the slow couple (there was always a slow couple) who suddenly decide to turn round or stop and had no indicators or brake lights to warn us, so we all bumped into each other, causing a log jam.

Next, we would walk into the couple who appeared to be paid by the cruise company to walk round the wrong way (there was always one of those too, despite arrows on the hull and fairly explicit instructions - please walk anticlockwise - and we always met them at the narrowest point). This couple were always about 90 if they were a day and walked along, side by side, holding all their cabin baggage in a holdall which must have weighed about five kilos by the look of it, plus a couple of towels, two or three books, a Kindle, a mobile phone into which they always seemed to be talking and an undrunk cup of tea full to the brim. In order to balance themselves, the arm not attached to the mobile phone would stick out sideways, making it impossible to pass. Seeing problems looming if we all continued to walk, we stopped while they tottered towards us, the tea slopping about a bit so we usually either got scalded or hit on the shoulder by a passing towel, elbow or book. This obstacle overcome (or at least passed), we continued, stepping over people resembling leatherback turtles who positioned themselves to catch the sun wherever it happened to be, including in the middle of the promenade, contorting their bodies to ensure that every square centimetre of it should come up to the mahogany standard. We had to be pretty vigilant of our surroundings, but the worst danger came from above.

The staff on many ships work twenty-four hours a day. Rumour has it that in order to work on a ship, all staff have to pass the "I don't need any sleep" test – if they need sleep, they don't get the job. The painters never stop painting. Equipped with white overalls, hard hats and goggles (night vision, obviously, at night), these intrepid workers paint. Their paintbrushes, sometimes as small as toothbrushes, are attached to fishing rods which can be as long as the height of two houses. The painters then abseil up the sides of the hull and paint over tiny spots of rust to preserve the pristine, super-white colour of the ship. Once up there, they are attached to the side of the ship and cannot see to come back down, so they bounce back, their feet seeking whatever hold they can on the lifeboat davits, the lifeboats themselves, the railings or the head or shoulders of a passing promenader. They have the fishing rod in one hand and the paint pail in the other. The instability of their perch can precipitate the paint pail to veer off the perpendicular and empty its contents onto the unwary below. This has not yet actually happened to us, or anyone we know, but it must only be a matter of time...

Of course, there were times when we had to go clockwise round the deck. Sometimes the front or the back of the deck was cordoned off because of high winds, inclement weather or maintenance and we would set out, the shuffleboarders shuffling, the quoiters quoiting, and hurry round to keep out of the line of fire. On these occasions, we always met someone coming the other way. We would do a dance, both moving to the same side, or both hanging back or running forward to keep out of each other's way. Inevitably, we ended up well and truly in each other's way, jogging into each other, or someone else who happened along at the wrong moment, and at least one cup of coffee would go flying. Continuing, we would avoid the couple who thought Dr Livingstone still had not been found, who would creep around the deck, binoculars to their eyes, with one and a half tons of Leica equipment round their necks, and a backpack with counterweights in to keep them from falling flat on their faces. They usually wore Tilley hats, sunglasses, Rohan jackets and serious cargo pants with hiking boots topping off (or bottoming off) the complete look. They never spoke to anyone, except each other, presumably. Hiking boots have never been an essential item for wearing on the promenade deck as far as we know; flip flops, bare feet and mules were always more prevalent.

Once, we met a young lady who seemed to have lost her skateboard. She was all dressed up in knee pads, elbow pads, wraparound sunglasses and trainers and fruitlessly ran up and down the same side of the deck. It was not between 0100 and 0600, but she ran for hours it seemed, and we wondered if she would do better running up and down on the other side, where there were some large trunks - maybe one had skateboards in it. Sometimes we were hit by a deck quoit and there would be cheers as it ricocheted off one of us and off the side of the ship. There must be hundreds of them around the huge left luggage office in the ocean which is Midway Island. After our allotted circuits we would give in – after all, we were on holiday.

21

THE BUGS BEGIN TO BITE

Back to the mystery cruise; Peter was taken ill half way through an excursion. We had had a bad outbreak of norovirus and the crew were taking no chances. We were not able to help ourselves to any food; it was all served to us. The programme we were given every day reminded us to wash our hands frequently, with hot water and soap and taking at least twenty seconds under the tap. Most people followed these instructions, but there were always those who would not. Mum used to put her hand under the antibacterial dispenser and take it away before anything had been dispensed. She would then rub her hands together as though she had antibacterialised them. We were not fooled. Others coughed without putting their hands over their mouths. Peter took tablets which reduced the acid in his stomach and made him susceptible to stomach bugs.

We were on the coach when he became ill. It was very sudden. The Trekkers rep was sitting across the aisle from us, and I told him Peter was ill. He immediately went to the front of the coach and asked if people would mind us going back to the ship and dropping off an ill passenger, then continuing the excursion. No one minded. The rep came back and phoned the ship. We would be met with a wheelchair and the doctor would be appraised of our arrival.

The Trekkers escort returned to his seat. Mum asked who was ill as he passed her seat, but he ignored her. She turned round to us.

'Who's ill?' she said,

'Peter,' I replied.

She took a good look at him 'Oh, my God, he looks terrible, has anyone taken his pulse?' she wailed, horrendously loudly. Everyone looked round. I ignored her. The coach turned round. It had to stop at every traffic light between town and port, but we arrived at the ship in minutes. The wheelchair was ready with two escorts, and Mum jumped up.

'Let these two off,' commanded the tour escort.

'But I'm his mother.'

'Let them off.'

She retreated.

'You can stay on the coach,' I suggested, 'finish the tour.'

'But I'm his mother!' the wails were getting even louder. She was determined to accompany us.

Peter was bundled into the wheelchair. I was right behind and behind me I could hear the tapping of mother-in-law's footsteps. I went faster; the footsteps went faster. She must have been running. She was talking non-stop to the second escort. I whispered in the ear of my escort, 'Please can you lose my mother-in-law?'

'Take the chair,' he said. I pushed the chair, going even faster now, and he dropped behind. I heard murmuring. He returned. 'Sadie is taking your mother-in-law for a coffee, there isn't room for all three of you at the doctor's.'

'Thank you, she just makes things worse.'

The doctor thought it was norovirus. He wasn't sure, but confined us to our cabin ALONE for 48 hours.

Peter was in bed and I was reading when the phone rang. We had been alone for about twenty minutes. It was Mum,

'I want to come and see Peter.'

'Sorry, no one is allowed in the cabin for 48 hours, and we aren't allowed out.'

'But I'm his mother.'

'He's trying to sleep, he needs quiet.'

'Can't I come to the door and look?'

'Not, now, perhaps later.'

'I want my lunch, are you coming?'

'No, I have to have room service.'

'So they go in the cabin.'

'No, they knock and leave it outside, covered with cling film.'

'Do I have to go into lunch on my own then?'

'I'm afraid so, yes, unless you have room service in your cabin.'

She disconnected.

A few minutes later, there was a knock on the door; it was Mum. She tried pushing past me, she tried looking over my shoulder. I hung on to the door and blocked the way. I thought of the times Peter had told me he was ill when he was little and she had ignored him; I thought of the odd times he had been ill since we had been married, and her complete lack of interest when I had let her know.

'Mum, we are in quarantine, you must go away, phone us if you want to speak to me,' I said.

'Will you be going on the trip tomorrow?'

'No, we will still be in quarantine.'

'I don't want to go on my own.'

'The tour escort will look after you, or you can stay on the ship.'

'But I want to go on the tour.'

'You will be looked after.'

'Will you be watching the show tonight?' She was still trying to look over my shoulder, but I was taller, the door was in the way, and the bed was not visible from where she was.

'We have to stay here and not go out for two days,' I said. 'No, I will not be watching the show.' I was beginning to wonder if Mum understood that 48 hours was the same as two days.

'I'm going to lunch now,' she said and was off.

We had no peace, but it was not norovirus and Peter soon recovered. After 48 hours we had earned our release.

Mum would get ill too. She would start off on a cruise eating everything in sight, with the mentality of 'I've paid for it so I am going to eat it,' a view shared by many. This would continue for two days, then she would be sick, usually after the evening meal. She would greet us the following morning.

'Oh, I have been so ill, it must have been something I ate, I must have eaten some herbs (she didn't eat herbs) or spices (she didn't eat spices) or sauce (she didn't eat anything runny, except custard or marie rose sauce) or that funny looking... (she didn't eat anything funny looking) or the foreign food (she didn't eat anything foreign) or anything beginning with H (honey, haricots verts, hummus and hollandaise sauce, as well as the herbs).Hake and haddock didn't count, as they started with F and neither did ham as it started with M. We never did tell her she had been greedy, but after two days she would eat less and remain well.

I was ill once; we all thought it was norovirus until one of my specimens proved otherwise. Before they knew what it was, people in bunny suits and masks had come in and sterilized the entire cabin and en suite. Once I was better, they did it all again. Ships earn reputations for being 'ill ships', but it is not the fault of the ship. They could not do more. Cleaners, like painters, never stop.

I was in the loo outside the entertainment lounge, actually in a cubicle, when there was a commotion outside the door. Someone had emerged and was not going to wash their hands.

'Aren't you going to wash your hands?' I heard.

'No, I am not,' came the rejoinder.

'That's disgusting,' came another voice, and yet another said, 'That's how we all get ill'.

'I'm not washing my hands,' I heard, and the door slammed. An animated discussion ensued, and the virtues of the newsletter and in-cabin video on norovirus were praised. The vigilance of staff who antibacterialise our hands when we enter communal rooms and the cleanliness of the ship were appraised. Someone's ears were also probably burning with the comments she received. I was only sorry that my skill of keeping people on one side of a door was not available to them. I might have stopped her leaving. The discussion was still going on when I came out. I washed my hands very thoroughly and left.

22

THE CAKEWALK, OR IS IT THE GANGPLANK?

The ship shops are lovely, particularly for women as they are usually stocked by women and have more for them. They are full of holiday essentials you never knew you needed; the toiletries you forgot or ran out of, birthday cards, anniversary cards and picture frames which make great presents for people you don't know very well and then lots of clothes, (mostly women's) handbags and jewellery. Mum went into the shop several times every day and even bought a Christmas present for us in there one year. (It wasn't the only present, I hasten to add.) There was a leather bookmark for each of us with details of the *Candy* on it. Unfortunately, there was a spelling mistake on it; instead of saying 'draught' it said 'daught'. We were not sure if it was pronounced 'daft'. She had left the price on the back - £1.00. Thanks Mum.

As well as working in the shop, the assistants worked as tour guides and held daily half-price sales (were the bookmarks actually 50p?) and the occasional fashion show, using the cruisers as models.

On this particular day, the cruisers were modelling formal and informal wear, all on sale in the ship boutique. What they had to do was not difficult. They started from the boutique, walked around the top of a glass effect spiral staircase, walked down the stairs, stopping at a landing for the cruise director to explain their apparel, then on to the bottom, out of view of everybody, up the main staircase (to leave the spiral stairs free for the next model) and back to the boutique for a grand finale with all of them together. Well, this would not normally have been too difficult, but the volunteers or boutique staff choices were the oldest and crumbliest of passengers.

It started with Horace from Northumberland, who enjoyed making models out of matchsticks. Geography did not appear to be one of his strong points at school; he had to be pointed in the right direction, lost his way even before approaching the stairs and eventually reached the top and stopped. He probably used a stair lift at home. He finally got to the halfway landing and came to a halt and after his commentary, he found it increasingly difficult to walk down the stairs. Ten minutes later (well, it seemed like it) he negotiated the bottom step and we all drew a breath of relief, including all the people arranged around the bottom of the steps, rather like trampoline spotters, laid on to lend a hand if he got stuck.

Next came Gertrude, who enjoyed gardening. She started off in pigeon step mode, looking intently at the ground; she seemed worried that it might disappear. Of course, when she got to the stairs, it did. Normally, she probably also had a stair lift and some reins, as she found the first landing with great difficulty. Clinging onto the rail for dear life, she inched her way down the stairs step by step, as a young child does. We waited, crossing our fingers that she would make it. Eventually she too found the bottom. Phew.

Daphne, who came next, was an entirely different type of person; confident, imposing and a great model. Her hobbies included watercolour painting, showing her dogs at Crufts and Zumba, but even she found it hard to negotiate the stairs when Gertrude decided to come back up (against all advice) holding onto both rails for dear life, and with white knuckles, and when she reached her, hanging onto Daphne as well. They looked like two women dancing from the Joyce Grenfell record, although neither lady was stately as a galleon. The fashion show limped on (literally) while one passenger, who had nothing to do with anything, decided to come up the stairs too. Not fazed by this in any way, the cruise director described what the passenger was wearing, but pointed out that it could not be bought in the boutique! The interloper wasn't fazed either. He did a nice neat twirl on the landing, taking off his jacket and walking off up the stairs with a wiggly bum, then twirling the jacket behind him and giving a cheery wave and a bow at the top of the stairs before he walked off into the distance. The applause for him was deafening, and there were a few whistles of appreciation as well.

We had roughly eight models and the whole show took about three quarters of an hour. At the end, as they were lining up outside the boutique, Gertrude was nowhere to be seen; rumour has it she was spotted later with the interloper, having a cup of coffee on deck. The dress she wore was reversible and her commentary included such advice as 'if you wear this at dinner and spill pudding all down you, all you have to do is take it off and hey presto, you have a new, clean dress'. And would Gertrude care to demonstrate? No, she definitely wouldn't. We hoped she could find the way to her mouth, or she might need that reversible dress.

23

SEA'S ROUGH

We all love whales – well, the Japanese don't, and the Chinese and the Norwegians don't, but we Brits love them. They are like Concorde and red kites (the birds, not the children's toys). No matter how many times I saw Concorde, I stopped and watched each time she flew overhead. We have red kites at home and I watch all of them as they swoop and glide above us. No matter how many whales I see, I want to see more.

We were up the St Lawrence River, where it meets the Saguernay River, a hotbed for Beluga whales. (They are the large, white ones, not easy to spot unless they want you to see them; they look like a cross between a bottlenose dolphin and a jumbo jet, and they have no dorsal fin.) We were reliably informed that we would definitely see them there.

We were due at the confluence at 16.20. We weren't doing anything else until then, so we went onto the balcony and watched and waited... and waited... and waited... 16.20 came and went, 1700 came and went. All we had seen were lots of white horses. We gave up and quickly showered and changed for dinner, cameras at the ready, an ear open for the call of 'whales!' from the captain.

We went into dinner, warning the maitre d. that if whales were seen we would be off, dinner getting cold or not. He didn't mind, he was used to it. It got dark. Definitely no whales. There are 10,000 of these whales in this area, so seeing them was a certainty, or so we had been told. We only wanted to see one, or perhaps two or three – not much to ask out of 10,000 is it?

Next day, most disgruntled, we went to the natural history lecture.

'How many of you saw the Beluga whales yesterday?' he asked. Some hands went up.

'We were lucky to see so many, and right on cue too, how many of you were out watching at twenty past four?' our hands went up.

'They were on both sides of the ship, but quite hard to spot. If you saw lots of white horses together, that was them, they cause the white horses and there is a shadow right underneath. It was a good show, you were lucky.'

I don't know what is worse, not seeing the whales, or not seeing them and then being told you had. I still maintain that I have never seen a Beluga whale.

We were cruising towards Iceland. It was breakfast time and the ship was about to dock.

'What are you doing today?' Peter asked our table companions.

'We're going whale watching,' they said.

'Wow,' I joined in, 'you must have booked early. There were only twelve places on that one.'

'I know, it's the highlight of our trip, it was very expensive, but we just love watching whales, and this is the place to come for them.'

'Have a lovely time,' we said as we left the table.

The sea had been very rough towards Iceland and I had been seasick, but I was quite happy that we were doing our own thing. As we went out, our cagoule hoods went up, it was pelting, the wind was icy and we could hardly speak as the wind took away our words. That evening we met our breakfast companions again.

'Hello, did you have a good day?' Peter asked.

'It was one of the worst days of my life,' she said.

'Let's have a drink,' I suggested, so we did that and listened to their tale of woe. They had gone out to the jetty just after breakfast as it was an eight-hour all-day trip (with a packed lunch). They were met by a little fishing boat - that was why only twelve could go. Unsurprisingly, it stank of fish. They climbed aboard, all of them in their wet gear as it was pouring with rain. They were given the choice of sitting upstairs in the open air getting wetter than ever, or going below in the dry but stinky cabin, but there wasn't room for them all to go to the same place.

Everyone eventually chose and settled and they set off. The sea was still incredibly rough and the fishy smell became combined with the delicate smell of the diesel motor - a potent combination which resulted in several passengers seeing their breakfast all over again. No one stayed settled; upstairs were the fumes and rain, downstairs were the fish, worse fumes and illness. Downstairs also had windows so steamed up they couldn't see out of them anyway. The boat heaved itself up and down the long swell, the passengers just heaved. No one wanted lunch, the crew brewed up tea and coffee, no one much wanted that either, apart from anything else, it was difficult to hold a beverage without spilling it over everyone aboard. The smell of coffee was added to the other smells and didn't smell appetizing. They bobbed up and down all day and saw - nothing.

They arrived back chilled to the bone with the smells still sticking to them. A shower and hair wash improved the position, but they didn't feel like dinner. We commiserated; there wasn't much else we could do.

The following day the sea calmed down, the winds lessened and the sun came out. Half way through the morning the captain said there were three whales on the starboard side playing and that as we had plenty of time, he would circle them so we could watch and photograph their antics. We had a wonderful display for about twenty minutes in the comfort of our own cabin and absolutely free of charge.

24

TOO MUCH OF THE DRINK

We went on a wine-tasting trip. Now these become more entertaining as the trip goes on, as many passengers feel this is a good opportunity to consume as much free wine as they can. It becomes especially jolly if several wineries are visited in succession.

On this particular trip we were visiting three wineries. The first was the oldest, a boutique winery, so no chance of buying its wines in the UK, and if you liked it, you had to get it down you fast, before we moved on. We tried three wines and continued to the largest vineyard in the area - five wines here. We were invited to take the last glass of wine up a hill which had a lovely view of the surrounding countryside. The last glass was a red. One woman wearing a white teeshirt (you already know what's coming, don't you?) could not wait to take a few snaps of the vineyard, and as she clicked the camera with both hands full, she managed to tip her glass of red and to flick lots of large spots of red wine down her ample breast. She then took the next five minutes trying to remove the stains, which slowly spread until she gave up. She arrived back at the winery with a pink and white teeshirt.

Some people drank all the wine, which was 15% proof (and the equivalent of four glasses with no lunch), while the rest of us had a sip and gave the rest to the plants. We then visited our final winery with more glasses on offer before returning to our coach. Some people became rather loud and found getting back on the coach rather a challenge. One lady sized up the door from all angles and banged into each side of it (she was just checking for size) before finally managing entry.

It started off quietly on the journey back, apart from inane giggling. It became noisier; maybe some keen members of the choir were practising, but we couldn't recognize what they were singing and eventually, it died out. The tour guide started reading poetry to us, and this was accompanied by more and more snoring as we arrived back at the dock.

We were given freebies on this tour: a jar of lemon myrtle jam and two bottles of wine, one white and one red. When we arrived back, it was raining, but we all waited docilely in the deluge to have our hands sanitized, submit our boarding cards for swiping, placed our bags through the contraband detector and ourselves through the metal detector.

Well, that's what we thought we'd do. It was what we usually do. The bottles of wine completely threw everything. You see, there is one big problem here. You can buy wine on the ship and they do not want you buying it anywhere else. We can see their point of view and have been through it before when we bought Curaçao in Curaçao for cousins in New Zealand when we visited them some years previously, but we had to hand it in and couldn't get it back until we arrived in the UK, so the cousins didn't get it.

As the first of the 44 people on the trip put their bottles through the contraband detector, pandemonium broke out. The bottles would have to be confiscated! The line came to an abrupt halt (spare a thought for those still waiting outside in the rain, desperately wanting to come aboard in the dry, not knowing what was happening) as the card swipers pondered what to do.

Reinforcements had to be sent for, pens that wrote had to be sent for, little cards had to be sent for, people who knew what they were doing had to be sent for (this took some time) and each bottle had to be recorded with the name of the accompanying passenger and the number of the cabin. We were not allowed to write our own, presumably in case we bequeathed our bottle to someone else, or borrowed their cabin number. Next the details had to be checked and verified (sounds like a telephone vote) – we were allowed to do that! Then it was reproduced on another card, one kept with the bottle, one kept with us and then we could go.

Unfortunately, the staff had not reckoned on pens running out of ink, labels being written incorrectly and the amount of alcohol already consumed as some people refused to give up their wine. Scuffles broke out, passengers and staff took sides and bottles were abused. The contraband detector gave up the ghost, the metal detector wilted, and wails were heard from the passengers left outside who thought they were missing out on a party and wanted life jackets as they were now beginning to drown in the rain. Eventually, after a few injuries (mostly to the bottles), things began to calm down. We escaped to our cabin without our wine. In all this, no one noticed the lemon myrtle jam, which got through without a fight. Technically, we are not allowed to bring any food aboard from land or to take any food from the ship onto land because of contamination locally, so the jam should have been impounded as well, but we were not saying anything.

Rumour has it that the doctor was very busy afterwards and they ran out of bandages, plaster of Paris, pain killers, Valium and salve. They had to repair all the machinery and clean the blood and wine stains off the carpet. We couldn't leave port until it was finished.

25

MUM CAN'T WAIT

Mum was the most extreme person I ever knew and the faddiest eater. Dad said she hated change so much that she wouldn't even move a chair, and the most impatient. Her self-indulgence showed itself the first time we met, in 1969.

'Does your mother go to the hairdresser?' she asked me.

'Yes,' I answered guardedly; I was already wary of her after only a few hours.

'I've never washed my hair since I got married,' she answered proudly. I thought of my own mother and my friends' mothers, with their home perms to save unnecessary expense after the war.

'Does your mother work?' the inquisition continued.

'Yes, she's a civil servant at the Ministry of Defence.' I was proud of what my mother did, and so was my mother, who enjoyed her work. She would have been bored stiff without it and the money certainly came in handy. She used to go off on her bicycle. Goodness knows what my mother-in-law would have thought of that!

'Oh, I've never worked, I don't need to. You make all your own clothes too, don't you?'

'Yes, so does my mother and most of my friends.' I was getting the hang of this. I wished I'd mentioned the bicycle.

'I buy all mine, I don't need to make them. I hate sewing.'

It continued in this vein, but I won't. She expected instant gratification, and with Dad, she got it. On a cruise, she had to wait in line with everyone else.

We were in St Petersburg, and if you have ever been there, you do not go to a public loo, you go with the rest of the tourists in a trinket shop. We had stopped in a trinket shop (Mum loved them) for the loo and a spot of shopping. We joined the end of the queue. There were about fifteen or sixteen ladies in front of us and as many of them were elderly, the queue was moving forward slowly. I was in front of Mum. This might seem rude, but there was a purpose to this.

We stood there for a minute or two without moving.

Mum huffed and inched forward, while I braced myself to stay put. She inched forward again, and now I could feel her handbag pushing into my back. I still stayed put. Had I moved forward, I would have been pushing into the lady in front of me. Now you know why I stood in front of her in queues. I had done this before, many times.

'What on earth are they doing in there?' she demanded, none too quietly, to titters from a few ladies ahead.

'What do you *think* they are doing?' I answered. More titters. She didn't answer, but she leaned on me. The bag was now pushing right across my back, and I still resisted. Someone came out, and we shuffled forward. The pressure on my back was relieved.

'However long are they taking in there?' she asked.

'No one stays in a public loo any longer than they have to,' I replied.

'How many toilets are there?'

'I have no idea, like you, I have never been here before.' I was getting waspish. She was leaning on me again, and the bag was back in my back. It was beginning to hurt.

'Three toilets, but one is out of order, and another doesn't lock. The third doesn't flush,' shouted someone for the front; she was obviously following our conversation.

'Thanks,' I trilled to the anonymous caller.

'I want to buy something. I won't have time. We'll

have to get back on the coach by the time we get to the front of the queue,' she whined. It was like being in a queue with a four-year-old. I ignored her, and she began to push me again. Her shoes were right against mine. If I had moved sideways, she would have fallen over (oh, the temptation!) We shuffled forward again and so on until we were at the front. I let her go in front of me then (you see, even I give in in the end) and off she toddled.

I came out before her, and when ready, I waited as she often got confused in new places. She took a long time, just as long as many others. She came straight out. I had to remind her to wash her hands, and she flapped a couple of fingers under the cold tap for about three seconds. I offered her my antibacterial foam. She pooh-poohed that and went out to explore the trinket shop.

Mum was now in her element. She preferred trinket shops and coffee shops to the rest of the excursion. More of that later.

26

WET BRIEFS AT DAWN

You can make friends or enemies for life at the laundrette. On one occasion we were told about, a foreign lady, not conversant with the British occupation of queuing, pushed in to grab an ironing board, ignoring three waiting people, and all hell let loose, skin and hair flying everywhere, with several acrylic fingernails found on the floor later.

I went to the laundrette one day just before it was due to open, at 8 am. There were already three in the queue, but that didn't matter, as there were eight machines. There was some chat about people who spent all day in the laundrette, and wasn't that sad, far better get it done early.

It got to past 8 am and I asked if anyone could pick a lock. The chap next to me said that it would be funny if while we had been standing outside the door had been open all the time. I suggested he try it. You've guessed it – it was open. Now we know what is sadder that staying in the laundrette all day, don't we?

We had a bad experience in the laundrette once. Peter showed a lady how to work the washing machines; in fact he did it all for her, put in the washing, turned on the machine, put the token in the slot, chose the programme and that was that. We were in there using the dryers and happened to be using the dryer above her washing machine. Later in the morning, I went back to take out the drying and put in some more. The same lady was there, taking out her washing and putting it into a basket ready to claim a dryer when one became vacant. I emptied the dryish clothes into a basket (the machine still had a few minutes to go) and started putting the wet clothes in it.

'You can't do that,' she said.

'Why not?' I replied,

'Because that's my dryer. I had the washing machine, so I take precedence over you.'

'I don't think so. Does anyone know what happens in situations like this?' I asked to no one in particular, but generally to the four or five other people in there. They all seemed very interested in their machines, ironing or the wall, and I had no reply.

'It's my dryer,' the lady continued, 'you can't have it.' She took out my clothes, shoving them into my chest. Trying not to fall backwards, I replaced the wet clothes in my bag, fuming. I had no choice but to let the lady use the dryer, as she had thrown her clothes in by then, and I went to reception to ask about rules in the laundrette.

'There aren't any,' explained the girl.

'So someone with a washing machine does not take precedence over someone just using the dryers?'

'Certainly not, it is first come, first served.'

'Thank you,' I smiled. I returned to the laundrette. It had emptied, and the woman was the only person in there.

'Next time you decide to make up rules about something of which you know nothing, just stop and check,' I said. 'I have been to reception and you had no right to take that machine. When someone is kind enough to help you, have a little grace,' I spat at her, 'and if I hear of you trying to intimidate or bully anybody else, there will be trouble.' I had no idea what kind of trouble, but thought it sounded good. She looked stunned, and I swept out.

Walking round the promenade deck during the next few days, it seemed as if all of the people present at our little fracas came up to us and commented on the unpleasant, ungrateful woman in the laundrette. Yes, you can definitely make friends or enemies for life.

27

A FISHY STORY

Barbara Cartland was dead; it had been on the news and everything. So how come we met her on a cruise? It was a loyalty club cruise, just open to those of us in the loyalty club. The club was divided into bronze, silver and gold. You added up the nights you spent on the ship and you earned points. We had reached the dizzy heights of silver. Gold had only just been invented, with just thirty members. Quite what the benefits of cruising with loyalty members were, we weren't quite sure, but the ports involved were interesting, and Mum liked the idea, so we booked.

It was the first evening and we were sitting at the

dining table with our table companions – well, to be more accurate, some of our table companions, as some hadn't arrived. It was a table for seven and five of us were making the usual sort of first evening small talk - have you travelled a long way? Have you been to these ports before? That sort of thing.

There were still two spaces to fill, so we asked the waiters to wait before bringing the first course, which we had already ordered. However, the spaces did not fill and in the end, thinking that maybe our companions were tired and missing dinner, we started.

Nearly an hour later, while we were finishing our main course, a couple emerged at the top of the staircase at one end of the dining room. She was large, wearing pink and fanning herself as she walked (the ship was fully air conditioned). Her male companion was half her size, trotting down the stairs behind her, trying to keep up and not having much luck. Something told me they were heading our way. I was not wrong. She steamed across the dining room like a windjammer in full sail, right hand fanning like mad. She arrived at the table, her husband (as we found out) panting behind her, and they sat down. The rest of us were engaged in a lively conversation on the relative merits of the various captains we had known, but it had to come to an untimely halt.

'Welcome to my table,' she gushed loudly, interrupting our conversation and our thoughts. 'I know you will have been vetted by Trekkers to come on our table and you will be our kind of people.' Five sets of eyes stared at her, five sets of eyes looked round at each other, five sets of eyes looked back at her. No facial expressions changed in the process, no words were spoken, only necks moved.

'Now, the process is this...' and she proceeded to deliver instructions to us on how we were to conduct ourselves at dinner in the evenings. She continued, informing us at the earliest opportunity that they were gold members and very highly thought of by the captains. Also, that as gold members they would be holding a soirée for thirty people one evening before dinner, and that if we were very good, we might just be invited. The pleasant chit chat between the five of us who arrived at the table together was completely overrun by this woman, who dominated the conversation all evening, occasionally being egged on by her husband saying, 'Barbara, tell them about the time...'

After pudding and beverage with petits fours, Mum decided her back was hurting and she had to get up. We followed and were followed quickly by our early companions, leaving Barbara and her husband still on their main course. It did seem a bit rude, but when Mum's back has had enough, the discomfort distresses her and we have to go.

The five of us agreed we would continue to start dinner when the dining room opened. 'After all,' said one of our companions. 'The waiters don't want to be waiting for us all night, they want to be laying up the tables for breakfast.'

Each evening, the five of us arrived promptly and enjoyed lively conversation on many topics. Each evening, Barbara, fan and husband would make a dramatic entrance an hour or so later. Each evening she would dominate conversation from then on. Each evening, Mum's back would play her up and five of us would leave together.

A few nights later, Barbara told us how much she loved music. 'I can't live without my music,' she declared, and she regaled us with a story of how she was walking through London one evening, prior to a concert by the London Philharmonic Orchestra. As she walked, a cab drew up alongside her and a voice said, 'Are you going to the concert? Hop in.' It was the conductor. She was nowhere near the concert hall, apparently, but somehow this person picked her out of all the pedestrians and knew exactly where she was bound. We were stupefied.

'Which instruments do you play?' I asked, taking the conversation back to her love of music. There was a pause, quite a long pause,

'The recorder,' she replied.

'In an early English ensemble?' I continued. She changed the subject.

The time came for their soirée for thirty, and the table was duly invited. Obviously we had all behaved ourselves and passed muster, although for some reason, Barbara refused to speak to Peter. She either ignored him completely, or spoke to him through someone else, usually Mum.

We arrived at the venue at the allotted time. Strange, with all the cruising they had done, Barbara and her husband didn't invite any other passengers, just the table and some of the higher ranking crew.

We got talking to the captain and he asked what I did, so I told him I helped out in an old people's home, and he replied, 'So do I'.

We knew about half a dozen of the gold members on the cruise and were very surprised they had not been invited. After half an hour or so, we went off to dinner. When Barbara arrived later, she sat next to Peter. She leaned across to him and conspiratorially said, 'Now you know how it's done.' After that she continued to ignore Peter again until one evening she was talking about the famous pianist John Lill. 'I went to school with him,' put in Peter, and he went on to name a few more famous names who had attended his alma mater. After that, Peter was her favourite.

The last evening arrived, not much time left for Barbara to hone our social skills, but still she tried.

'You bronze lot,' she opened, but by this time someone had had enough, and was going to correct her,

'Actually Barbara, we are all silver on this table, apart from you two, of course.'

Her mouth opened, then closed and she went quiet.

28

MUM VISITS THE CROW'S NEST

We were in Marseilles, a panoramic coach drive as Mum's walking was now quite poor. She had had her disabled badge for several years and this was to be her final cruise, although we didn't know it at the time.

We left the ship on a coach, stopping about fifteen minutes later for a photo stop at the bottom of the steps to the church of Notre Dame de la Garde, the highest point in Marseilles, looking out over the sea to Chateau d' If, fictional prison of the Count of Monte Cristo. The tour guide suggested we stop for ten minutes, and the most energetic of us could trot up the 200 steps up to the church for an even better view. She asked if anyone wanted to go up the steps; Peter and I were the only ones interested. Mum told us she was staying on the bus. The tour guide said they would wait for us, but that we should be as quick as possible, and we agreed we would go as fast as we could, as we didn't want to keep everyone waiting. She went on to mention there were lavatories at the top too.

We got up for the photo stop, but Mum, to our surprise, got up too.

'We're going up to the top Mum, you may as well stay on the coach,' I said.

'I'm coming with you,' she insisted.

'But we're going up 200 steps, you can't do that.'

'I want to go to the toilet.'

'They are at the top of the steps, you'll never make it. We only have ten minutes.'

'I am coming with you, I want to go to the toilet.'

'But it's 200 steps, that's 200 up and 200 down, a total of 400.'

'I don't care, I'm coming with you.'

Mum had been to the loo just before leaving the ship, about twenty minutes before. She hadn't thought about it until the guide mentioned the word, but psychological or not, if she was uncomfortable and needed the loo, we would have to take her. There was no way round it; we couldn't have her uncomfortable and unable to concentrate for the next three hours.

Peter and I looked at each other. 'I'll tell the guide Mum will take longer than ten minutes, and I will go

up with Mum,' I said. 'You go on up before us, take some photos and find out where the loo is, so we can get up and back as soon as possible.' He nodded and ran on ahead up the steps. The guide was brilliant, 'Just get back as soon as you can,' she said.

Gratefully, I started up the steps with Mum. Peter by this time was out of sight. We clambered up those steps, and Mum got slower and slower. Eventually, near the top, we met Peter coming down to meet us. He had taken some photos; it was my turn now. I ran on ahead and staked out the loos, to make sure Mum would cope with doors, flushes and taps. So far, we had taken twenty minutes.

Peter and Mum were now at the top and I showed her into the loo. Peter then suggested I went into the church to take some photos (he had taken the view) while Mum was in the loo. I ran off, just as two other women from the coach arrived.

While I was off taking photos, Mum started making a wailing noise from the loo. 'Where is the light? It's dark in here, I can't find my way.' Peter had to ask the ladies if they could help Mum. They were delighted, and very helpful. We were grateful that they had changed their minds about coming up.

I came out of the church as Mum was being helped out of the loo. The ladies and Peter went on down the steps, Peter to let the guide know how long we would be. I went down with Mum, slowly now as she had had enough. She stopped about half way down.

'What a nice view,' she said and stood and looked, quite unaware of the time constraint.

'Come on Mum, we've got to get back quickly, the whole coach is waiting for us,' I said. I was thinking of what kind of reception we would get, arriving back so late at the start of the tour. To be fair, she did start to trot down the stairs again. Eventually we arrived at the last flight of steps, just twenty more stairs to descend. Then at last we were at the bottom. The Trekkers guide was waiting for us, while everyone else was on the coach and ready to go.

'Are you all right, Lilian?' he asked.

'Oh, I don't know how I did it. If someone had told me how many steps there were, I wouldn't have gone,' she wailed.

Just how many times had she been told? He helped her up the steps of the coach, while I stood in impotent frustration at the bottom, my mouth opening and closing silently (we have goldfish at home; I was clearly becoming like my pets). Mum disappeared down the aisle.

'I know,' he put his hand on my shoulder, 'I had a mother-in-law like Lilian too.'

29

WATER SPORTS

Do you remember the 2013 Olympics? I do, I was an Olympian and although I didn't earn a medal, I earned a coolbag and a certificate. Okay, so you have realized I don't mean the 2012 Olympics, but the 2013 Olympics were just as exciting. I represented Mexico, as our team leader lived in Mexico for a while, his daughter was born there and he spoke Spanish. I wasn't going to argue as my godson lived in Mexico for a year and we boarded this particular cruise in Acapulco, so it was all good.

Peter was a bit under the weather, so I had to do this alone – well, not quite alone, there were four of us in the team and there were thirteen teams. My ideas on the Olympics on a ship were that maybe we would have a relay race round the promenade deck (anticlockwise, of course) or shot put with melons, but I was wrong.

The first game was golf. Now I have never played golf, or wanted to, so this was going to be tricky. I changed into my Mexican sports outfit and in so doing, tried to intimidate the opposition. Ah. For golf, read carpet bowls, another game I have never played. No one was wearing uniform, so I just looked a bit stupid. Never mind, my bowling would do the talking.

We started off. I have no idea of scoring or anything, but we were slightly behind when it came to my turn. I, for some reason, had been chosen to go last.

'Something tells me you are going to be really good,' remarked the organizer (not Sebastian Coe). I must have pulled a face or something, as everyone laughed. I tried to look impressive as I brought my arm back and let go the little black ball. It toddled along the carpet, coming to rest right beside the even smaller white ball. This, apparently, was what it was supposed to do. Right, now I knew, so I bowled another ball, and this did exactly the same thing. We had two rounds of this, and in the second round it happened again! Mexico had won against the others! Group hug, high fives and general patting on the back - not all at once, you understand, we didn't have enough arms for that.

Wii sport came next, in the guise of ten pin

bowling. I had never done this, either, so I was given a quick practice, as apparently there is a knack to it, and I mean quick. I practised once. I was not good. Only one of our team had ever played on a Wii, so we didn't do so well. At the end of day one, we were fourth.

Our next round was on April Fools' Day, so that sounded very encouraging. Doubles in shuffleboard which I had played before – trouble was, so had everyone else. The other couple representing Mexico were knocked out in the first round, but my partner and I reached the semi-final, coming joint third.

In the afternoon it was quoits and darts. Not such good news. My partner and I went out in the first round of quoits with the highest losing score and the smallest margin against the eventual winners. We felt we had done well and the other two did about the same. The quoits varied; some were rigid and went like the wind and others were floppy and needed some welly so there was much inconsistency and the quoits kept ending up where they shouldn't, which raised a few eyebrows and ruffled a few feathers.

Darts were played on an individual basis; you just had to gain a higher score than the person before you, so there was some luck too. The Mexicans soon showed they had not had a misspent youth in the pub, so they didn't do brilliantly. The eventual winner was the organizer (who had also won the Wii), who had joined a team to make up numbers - a bit of muttering ensued, although it was good natured (we thought).

Organizing the deck games on a daily basis does give a person just a small advantage.

Going into the last day, Mexico was in second place behind GB (the organiser's team), but we made a terrible hash of the general knowledge quiz and Mexico came third. We did make one silly blunder by giving the answer 'The rumble in the jungle' which should have been 'The thriller in Manila'. Again, no misspent youth fighting!

The final event, and we were either top or second with table tennis to play. Peter gave me some practice by having a knock-up with me beforehand, only the table had no net. It's much easier without a net – we are quite surprised it hasn't caught on. When the table tennis started, our captain put the stronger two together, and the weaker two (scientifically done thus - 'Are you any good?' so 'yes' came top, 'okay' came second and 'haven't played for ages' came third). The strong pair kicked off and lost 2-11 in the first round. My partner and I won the first round... and the second... and the third... and were knocked out 9-11 in the semi-final. My partner individually was 4th and I was 9th overall. Guess who won? Yes, the organizer. More muttering, not quite so kindly this time.

An award ceremony was held in the evening. The Mexican team came second after GB. I came 9th overall out of 52, the second placed female. As a team, we each had a cool bag and a certificate to say we had participated in 'The Beeline Beauty Olympics' which made it sound like the highland games. These were presented by one of the real Olympic torchbearers. Peter came to the ceremony as my coach, psychologist, sports scientist, manager, agent, trainer, mentor and thoroughly good egg. It was lots of fun and the first time I had been in an octothon.

30

FLOTSAM AND JETSAM

Mum's Christmas and birthday presents were legendary. The most memorable birthday present I had was quite incredible: three pairs of passion-killer knickers, two sizes too big, accompanied by a pair of rubber gloves - both left-handed.

I asked Peter if he thought his mother thought I was kinky. He stayed silent. He does that, it's less dangerous. Peter received three first aid kits in four years; Mum must have thought we were going through an accident prone patch. He also had a very strange gift of a block with a pencil and measure attached, but Mum freely admitted she had no idea what it was.

Charity shops did well out of us after Christmas, but one year she told us, 'You'll like your presents this year, I haven't bought you any rubbish,' and she hadn't – it was the only year the charity shops missed out.

One Christmas Dad was instructed to buy her a purse. He was told it was the one in the bottom right hand corner of the window of a shop in their local High Street. He duly went out, bought it, wrapped it and left it under the Christmas tree for her. On Christmas morning we were all opening our presents. Mum opened the present of the purse.

'I don't want this one, this isn't the one I told you to get; I like the sort that fold over. Take this back and change it.'

'I'll change it as soon as the shop opens after the holiday,' he said. 'I'm sorry, I must have misunderstood.' she chuntered on for ages about him. It was a tense afternoon.

She bought predictable presents for all her friends; for the ladies, either a tea towel or an oven glove, for the men a biro in a plastic box. It didn't matter what the biro was like, as long as it was in a box. She would frequently buy these when on holiday and they would be enhanced by the words 'A present from... wherever'.

We were with Mum in Ireland at a trinket shop selling Irish linen. 'Roslin, come here,' she shouted at me as I was admiring some embroidery, 'how much does this cost?'

I trotted over. She was holding a set of three tea towels.

'Not more tea towels for your friends? They could probably wrap all their Christmas presents up in your tea towels, they've got so many,' I said.

'No, no I just wanted to know,' and she walked away.

Thank goodness, I had stalled her. I always felt guilty when she bought her awful presents with us. I felt her friends must think Peter and I encouraged her.

'Roslin, come here,' she was shouting again, and in another corner looking at something else.

'What is it?' I asked.

'Do you think Sue would like this?' Another tea towel, this time a Delft lookalike in blue and white. Sue was our sister-in-law.

'I don't think her kitchen is blue,' I said.

'Doesn't matter, it's the thought that counts.'

She bought the tea towel and I apologized to Sue when we arrived home.

We were with Mum in St Petersburg at a trinket shop selling Russian artefacts.

'Roslin, come here,' she said, this time pulling at my sleeve as I was quite close. 'Do you think the girls would like these?' The girls were our nieces, Geoffrey and Sue's children, Claire, Jennifer and Eleanor. 'These' were tiny boxes, the size of a stamp, decorated with transfers. They were very cheap. There were prettier boxes behind them with more attractive transfers, several times larger, which would mean they could actually be useful and they were just over twice the price. They were also in the traditional black outside and red inside.

'I'm not spending that on them, there are three of them,' she said.

She bought the cheaper boxes and I apologized to Sue when we arrived home.

We were with Mum in Norway on a tour to visit a glacier. We left the bus and started to walk to the most amazing turquoise-coloured glacier which was a couple of hundred metres away. We walked past a trinket shop at the side of the path.

'I don't want to see the glacier' said Mum as soon as she laid eyes on the shop. 'I'll go in the shop and meet you when you get back.'

On our return Mum had a bag bulging with trinkets. I just hoped they weren't too awful. She suggested we had a coffee in the coffee shop which was in a corner of a glacier museum, so she sat down as Peter and I looked at the museum. She was perfectly happy. We had time to see a huge waterfall, one of the highest in Europe, which was another short walk away, but she wasn't interested in that either. Dad used to say Mum had no soul; she couldn't appreciate natural phenomena or the achievements of man, whether great or small. Mum wasn't even interested in the pyramids. She would have preferred to walk round Marks and Spencer.

31

MAELSTROM

We left Southampton to cruise straight across the Atlantic to the eastern seaboard of Canada to visit both English and French-speaking towns. It was early autumn – great for the colours of the trees, not so great for avoiding hurricanes.

The Captain's welcome party on the first night of this cruise gave him the opportunity to let us know we were not going where we thought we were. He showed a map of our route which had two huge yellow cauliflowers on it, one off the Florida coast and one further north and slightly further out into the Atlantic.

'These beauties ' he said pointing at the

cauliflowers, 'are hurricanes, Leslie and Michael, and they are moving at different speeds. They will meet and become one huge hurricane and arrive in Halifax, Nova Scotia just as we get there.' This sobering thought led to murmurs around the room.

'So, we are changing course, and instead of going straight across the Atlantic, we are stopping at the Azores. We will then follow the hurricane, but miss out Halifax. Head Office are at this moment changing the itinerary for us. Your original excursion money will be refunded and we will let you know what we are doing about new excursions instead. Enjoy the rest of the evening and I will keep you further informed in the morning.'

Chatting broke out all around as we thought about the situation. I was delighted, as I had been ill the last time we had been to the Azores and I could make up for lost time. Some people had already started the head beating: 'If I had only known we would not get to Halifax, I would not have come on this cruise'.

The following day, as if to make up for people's disappointment, a pod of whales caught up with the ship and showed off for an hour on the starboard side. We watched them from our balcony and loved every minute.

The weather was beautiful; hurricanes were far from our minds as we arrived in the Azores. Peter and I experienced a wonderful day on an island on which we had previously missed out. Our excursion took us to the top of an old caldera looking out over two beautiful lakes, said to have been formed from the tears of a green-eyed shepherd boy and a blue-eyed princess who could not marry. United at last, the blue of one lake and the green of the other looked tranquil and inviting on this warm and sunny day.

Back at the ship, however, some were not so happy. Landing on an island they did not wish to visit, they had chosen another excursion to a different caldera which was covered in mist, so they had seen nothing. Not a great first tour.

That night, at last en route for Canada, the captain spoke to us again and our route had once again changed; we were now missing out Gaspé, a small town in the French-speaking part of Canada. Arrangements had also changed in Sydney, Nova Scotia. We were still going there (a sigh of relief from the people with friends in Sydney), but instead of having a berth, we would now have to take the lifeboats and tender in instead.

After more days at sea, and having avoided all the bad weather, we arrived in Sydney. Tendering is always time consuming, but potentially fun, and with no tendering for a few days, the crew had to learn how to pilot the tenders all over again.

We were greeted at the port by a lone piper. Not to everybody's taste, the piper. We then had a lovely walk around Sydney which took a couple of hours and was at no time further away from the front than 100 metres, we could see the ship from all angles, we could hear the piper from inside the houses and we wondered just how much more they could squeeze out of such a little village. Even more than the piper was able to squeeze out of his pipes. We loved Canada and experienced the most incredible welcomes everywhere. One of our favourites was Trois Rivières in French-speaking Canada, where we were the very first cruise ship ever to berth there. The whole village, including pets, came out to see us off after befriending us during the day. The feeling could never be repeated.

Returning home down the St Lawrence River after calls at other towns and villages, we heard the captain again. 'We are going to Gaspé after all, but we are not stopping. We have a medical emergency and the person has to be medevacked off the ship. It is too foggy for the helicopter, so the coastguard will come alongside and we will more or less stop for a few minutes while the patient is removed. You are to sit down as the ship will be very unstable at that point.'

So like the people on the other tour in the Azores, we arrived at Gaspé and saw nothing.

Back in the Atlantic on another ship we also went round in circles. We were to have docked in La Palma, the island the furthest west in the Canaries, with the huge observatory on it, and it is notoriously difficult to berth there as the harbour at the port of Santa Cruz is susceptible to the strong Atlantic winds. Before we arrived in the area, the ship was already rocking and rolling on a long swell of over five metres and winds of upwards of 40 knots. Eventually, the captain had no choice. The winds were heading straight into the harbour, making it so dangerous to land that he decided to make for the next destination, Las Palmas town on Gran Canaria island (the Spanish are not very imaginative when it comes to place names) so we changed course...

A little later, with us all dressed in our finery for a formal evening, the captain told us we were not now going to Las Palmas as we had a medical emergency on board and we were now making for the nearest hospital, which was back at Santa Cruz on La Palma. We were to be met by a helicopter to medevac the patient off the ship (not easy given the conditions). The ship would have to almost stop to help the helicopter pilot and we would feel even more rolling at that point, so would we all please sit still (difficult unless he told us exactly when the helicopter was to arrive). So, we changed course...

A little later and the captain came on again to let us know the lady was safely off the ship, so we changed course...

A lot later, and in the middle of the night, with me unable to sleep for all the creaks, groans, swooshes and the occasional THUMP as we hit a wave made of steel, there was a decided THWACK somewhere in the cabin. Something had fallen somewhere. Just in case it was important, I woke Peter, who was not thrilled as he had only just managed to get to sleep. He did a quick inspection, but couldn't find anything wrong, and with everything in its place, he went off to sleep again, I stayed awake, in case we changed course again...

So, although we missed Gaspé in Canada, someone from the ship did arrive there and although we missed La Palma in the Canaries, someone from the ship arrived there, too.

32

THE TITANIC – AN ALTERNATIVE VERSION

When we were in Foynes in Ireland, we visited the Flying Boat Museum; we had never seen a flying boat, but we had heard all about them from one of the on board lecturers. Full of anticipation, we waited outside until the museum opened. Mum wasn't so interested, but there was a coffee shop and she thought she might wait there and let us look round.

The doors opened and we were let inside. All sorts of craft were in the museum, and there were mock-ups and posters, artefacts from flying boats, menus, the crockery, that sort of thing; it must have been so luxurious. We wandered around enjoying the atmosphere. We couldn't see a flying boat anywhere.

'Where are the flying boats?' we asked an official,

'We don't actually have one. We're reconstructing one, but we haven't finished, so it isn't on display. We'll have it in a year or two.'

We had visited a flying boat museum with no flying boat!

Back in Cobh in Ireland, and we were off to see the newly-developed Titanic Museum; it was 2012 and the centenary of the disaster had just passed. The redevelopment took place to coincide with this landmark time.

We went inside. It was a beautiful museum which had reconstructed parts of the ship. We picked up passes that had belonged originally to travellers on the Titanic and we could refer to parts of the museum to find out what happened to our characters (Peter's died, mine survived). The museum was interactive and went through the cruise, until it came to the sinking; at this point we were supposed to sit in a lifeboat mock-up and watch the liner as it sank below the waves, but it didn't sink. We looked at each other. Surely this was a story to which we knew the ending? And it wasn't people sitting in lifeboats for the fun of it, looking at their erstwhile home. We definitely knew better, or worse, whichever way you looked at it. After all, Peter's character was about to drown and he didn't jump overboard. He stayed on board. That was the problem.

'Oh, sorry ' said an official, 'that part of the museum doesn't work, you will just have to imagine it.'

We had visited a Titanic museum where the Titanic doesn't sink!

33

THE FOGHORN

I cannot guarantee you comfortable nights on board a ship. You may sleep like a baby all cruise, it has happened, you may be lucky, but there are too many variables of the noisy kind and the movable variety. I can however guarantee when you will not sleep – now that is a different matter. Keeping you awake is the prerogative of the crew, and if you need to be kept awake, well, tough.

You can make it easier, however. Look at the plan of the ship carefully before you book and if you aren't sure, speak to someone who knows the layout. Never book a cabin near the bridge; this is where the foghorn is kept and it is a law at sea that in conditions where you can't visually see where you are going (the captain always sees where he is going, even if you don't) this must be sounded. Usually it is foggy at night and if necessary, the foghorn will go all night. Be warned. The trouble is, often the best cabins are near the bridge. Book a cabin where you can see what is next door - another cabin is good. Avoid the lifts, not that they make much noise, but their occupants can, and do, usually at three o'clock in the morning when they all say 'good night' outside your door. Avoid what looks like a cupboard on the plan, it might be a 'steward's locker' and believe me, they can make a racket. I'm not sure if it is because they are trying to get out or in, but avoid it. And never, never go near the laundrette.

Having said all that, you still get foghorns. We had a really pleasant group of friends in the dining room. We sat at designated tables at a designated time and thoroughly enjoyed the experience. Just behind us was a table for eight which was kept for cruisers who wanted to dine 'free flow', coming in when they wanted and eating with whoever turned up at the same time. It worked well. Next to Peter with us, sat deaf Ethel, or deaf Eth to us. Deaf Eth knew she was deaf, she had hearing aids, but something was wrong with them (no, not the battery, that would have been easy) – she had problems hearing any normal speech at 60 decibels, so when she wanted to talk, she leaned over to Peter and spoke rather loudly into his ear.

This was fine until one evening the Foghorn sat behind us. She was cruising with a friend we called the Mute, as no one had ever heard her speak. The Foghorn sat at the table and introduced herself - to the entire dining room. Her strident tones shook the walls and went through us like a train whistle at about 90 decibels. She must have been a scout leader in a previous life. Deaf Eth cringed,

'Oh my God, what on earth was that?' she couldn't believe her ears.

It got worse. Unfortunately something made the Foghorn laugh. It interrupted conversations everywhere and was actually quite painful. We endured this for one dinner and hoped to goodness she wouldn't be back - she wasn't.

We followed the Foghorn and the Mute out of the dining room, and our route to our cabin took us past theirs. It was sandwiched between some offices on one side and the lift on the other. No cabins anywhere near. We wondered if when she had booked, the booking receptionist had said to her (no doubt regretfully) that they had absolutely no other cabins on the ship available.

34

THOUGHT READING

Mum was in the entertainment lounge earlier than we were. She was at the front, we were at the back, our usual place if there was any possibility of audience participation. The thought reader, Mystic Mick, our entertainment for the evening, was getting well into his act. He had correctly predicted the card someone would choose from a pack, the colour of scarf another person chose, and the name of an elderly lady's next door neighbour's dog.

'I need some help with this one. Now, who looks like a likely candidate? You, the gentleman over there with the green checked shirt. Are you a cowboy? No?

Good, a lumberjack? No, you wear the uniform well. Will you help me? What's your name?'

'You should already know it, shouted a wag from the back, 'you're a thought reader.'

'Just checking,' Mystic Mick came back, but Fred had already told him his name. 'Fred, I'm going to give you a book, look, here it is,' and he held up a book about as big as the Encyclopaedia Britannica if it had all been in one volume. 'I want you to choose a word on a page. Tell me the number of the page and I will guess the word.'

'Right,' said Fred and took the book. He riffled through it for a few seconds and said,

'I've got one, "traffic".'

'No Fred,' came the response, 'you find a word, tell me the page and I tell YOU the word.'

'Right,' said Fred and he resumed riffling. 'Balcony!' he shouted triumphantly. Laughs from around.

'No, no,' Mystic Mick shook his head, trying to keep us with him. I tell YOU the WORD, YOU only tell ME the PAGE,'

Fred's neighbour tried to help, there was much muttering, 'Right,' said Fred, more riffling, 'I've got one...'

'Don't tell me, don't tell me, don't tell me!' Mystic Mick, with arms waving, was getting quicker and louder and more excited each time he said it. 'Tell me the page, only the page.'

'120,' called Fred,

'What letter does the word start with, and I'll tell you which word.'

'X,' replied Fred,

Peter and I looked at each other, pretty easy that. It had to be x-ray, there wasn't much else beginning with x, unless it was a science book.

The entertainer wasn't so sure 'Are you sure it's X?' he asked, 'I don't think there are any words on page 120 beginning with X.' Oh, we thought, not so easy then.

'Yes, it's definitely X,' said Fred,

'Sorry, you are going to have to tell me,' Mystic Mick shook his head, mystified.

'Matrix,' shouted Fred confidently. Amid great laughter, Mystic Mick took the book from Fred and walked back to the stage. He caught sight of Mum, sitting there innocently,

'Hello, and what is your name?' he asked. (You see he still couldn't read people's names!)

'Lilian.'

'Would you like to try, Lilian? Take the book and find a word, then tell me the page it's on, but don't tell me the word,' he gave her the book and walked a few paces back to the stage,

'Now, Lilian,' he began, 'Lilian? Lilian?'

But inexplicably, Mum had dropped off to sleep.

35

BINGO

Bingo is not Peter's or my game, although when we were on a river cruise down the Nile he did win me a beautiful gold scarab beetle pendant, which I always wear. Not to be outdone, Mum won a beautiful gold Nefertiti pendant in the same game, which she unfortunately never wore.

The cruise director on this particular cruise, where people could be over seventy-five years of age, could be a little condescending on occasions when all the passengers were together, which was strange as she was never like that with individuals. It was evening, just before the show, and Mum had come in early to bag a good seat. We had told her not to worry about us; we had a problem with the water in our cabin and would have to wait for the plumber and might be late.

We arrived just as a game of bingo started. We didn't have a card, but we squeezed in at the back and sat and watched. The cruise director was explaining the rules slowly and with the intonation of an infants' school teacher with a particularly slow, hard of hearing class.

'Have you all got a bingo score card? If not, put up your hand and someone will give you one. What was that? No, you don't need pencils in this game, no. I said you didn't. OK, now, if you all have your cards ready, you will see that each number is uncovered. If you have any covered numbers, pull the little flap back until you can see them all. No, just pull them across, that's right. Have you all done that? Good. OK – no not everyone has done it, OK, I'll wait. All done now? Good.'

The cards were splendid; two stiff cards glued together with little windows for each very clearly printed number, all the windows shut with little metal edges which stood slightly proud of the card. Very clever, and they would last a long time.

'Now, have a good look at your card. You have BINGO written across the top of your card and five columns of numbers underneath, the first under the B, the second under the I and so on. OK? As I call out a number, if you have it on your card, shut the shutter across the relevant number, it goes from left to right. OK? We are playing for a full house, that means we are playing for a complete card to be full; all shutters shut across your numbers, you won't be able to see the numbers, just the shutters. If you fill your card and can only see shutters, you must call out bingo, or house, or Geronimo, or something to make yourself known BEFORE I CALL THE NEXT NUMBER. OK? I will then verify the numbers by reading them out, identifying which line they are in, so for instance, 12 under the B, 27 under the I and so on. OK? Any questions? No? OK, off we go.'

She read out about ten numbers and someone shouted 'Bingo!'

'Are you sure?' she asked, astonished, as there were more than ten windows to be closed.

'Yes,' said the claimant, I've got all the letters under the G.'

'Ah,' the cruise director replied, 'but we are playing for a full house, aren't we, not just a line, sorry, but we'll have to keep going,' and off she went again.

About six numbers later, 'Bingo!' shouted an anonymous voice in the corner.

'Are you quite sure?' she asked.

'Yes, I've got the third line down.'

'No,' she explained patiently, 'we are playing for a full house, not a line, I'm calling out again.'

By this time there were a few giggles, so order had to be reimposed. The gigglers hushed. The number calling continued. Eventually, someone called, 'Bingo! I've got a full house.'

'Thank goodness for that,' commented a chap along from us, who, like us wasn't playing. The numbers were checked. No, he'd made a mistake, he'd got 80, not 18, and off she went again.

I believe someone did win, in the end, and we now knew why she could be a little condescending.

36

MILITARY PRECISION

The Algerians were taking no chances. We were a shifty looking lot of seniors; who knew what we could bring into the country? Swine 'flu, for example, was doing the rounds and they didn't want to catch it. So before disembarking, temperatures were taken and irises scanned. Not having had our best features photographed, we clearly still looked shifty as our coach was completely surrounded by police. The excursion was a panoramic of Algiers, Mum's choice.

Looking from our balcony earlier, the city stretched out to the east and west, the ship being roughly in the middle. We could see our first stop out to the left at the back of the city way up on the hillside, the monument to the people who died in the fight for independence. The last stop was right over to the right, a Roman Catholic Church, also high up at the back of the city. We would have some great views to remember and photos to take back. We did not stay on the balcony long, as binoculars were not allowed and cameras were frowned on in the dock area. It was also drizzling; not what we expected in a North African capital.

Oh, perhaps they liked us after all? As we left the ship, the police, now accompanied by what looked like the army (it later transpired that the Algerians have country police and city police and we had earned both), formed a guard of honour between the gangway and the coach, which was about five metres away. We even had a red carpet! Except that it wasn't red, but green and mud coloured and it wasn't a carpet, but one of those dirt attractors you step on when you visit a farm with foot and mouth and you've already been through the disinfectant.

The coach must have been built some time between the two world wars. The bench seats were slippery with dark green shiny plastic so you slid about going round corners, and no need for anyone to clean them; we gave them a jolly good polish. There was also a chrome rail along the tops of the seat backs in front of you that you could hang onto if you got frightened. No seatbelts, no sick bags, no middle entrance, no air conditioning, no TV, no loo. This was definitely the Easy Jet of coaches, no frills.

As we climbed aboard, we noticed lots of motorbikes. The coach seemed to have pulled up at a motorcycle park, which seemed a bit inconsiderate, but there you are. We sat down. We had to carry our passports; we were identified and counted once inside the dock and again outside the dock, where we discovered a third type of police, the dock police, so we met them too.

Out of the dock, the coach took off like a Bugatti Veyron on rocket fuel. We slid back, our heads hit the metal back rest and we were flung forwards to hit them on the rail in front of us. We looked at each other dazed, the world spinning.

'Look out of the window,' said Peter. He was always on the window side as his camera took better pictures than mine when we were moving. Perhaps I should say he took better pictures than I did when we were moving. I looked out and saw outriders on bikes in front and behind the coach and in the very front was a police car, siren sirening and lights flashing.

'Are they going to lock us up? What's going on?' I didn't expect an answer, it was just something to say. It was unnerving. Another police car had joined us at the back and in the front car, a policeman was now hanging out of the door on the near side, flapping his arm about and waving traffic out of the way. By now we seemed to be doing about 90mph. I was starting to feel queasy. I remembered no sick bags. Never mind, I was always prepared.

We started down a dual carriageway and the local tour guide began to talk.

'We are going past the hospital and visiting time is just starting, so it is very busy right now, but don't worry,' he said. Don't worry? Who was he kidding?

Suddenly we lurched across the road, really, really across the road, and through a gap in the central reservation, where we continued on our way on the wrong side of the carriageway. It was completely clear. On the side we should have been on, the traffic was stationary, in fact, apart from our coach, we hadn't seen anything move in Algiers at all.

We tore down the road until we came to another gap in the central reservation, when we were flung to one side of our seats. Only a couple of people actually fell out into the aisle, which we thought wasn't bad, considering. A policeman was holding up the traffic on our old side (the wrong side) and the new side (the proper side) was clear of all traffic again. We slewed back the other way, and I hung on in order to stay on the seat. We belted down the road, the policeman in front clearing the way as we caught up with the afternoon traffic waiting to get into the hospital. They would have a long wait - we had to come back yet! My queasiness completely cleared as I hung on for dear life to the bar in front.

Back and forth we tore across the dual carriageway until we neared the monument. Inconsiderately, this had been built beside an ordinary road which was totally clogged by cars, minibuses, trucks and motorbikes, all hooting at each other. We were going to have to wait – well that's what we thought. The policeman in front had other ideas. He drove straight at the conglomeration of vehicles. He was mostly hanging out of the car now, his whole torso out of the door, arm waving madly at everyone in general, and do you know? They moved. It was amazing. Out of this huge pile, a path emerged and we flew along it to the monument. We had arrived, and most of us were still in one piece; in shock, but in one piece.

It was raining, and if there was one kind of weather Mum hated it was rain. She was proud of her hair, having it tinted and permed regularly, and she hated to wear a hat. Unfortunately, she was also lethal with an umbrella.

'I'm not getting out,' she announced.

'There's a good view from the monument,' Peter encouraged her.

'No, I'll stay here,' she said, and she was not to be moved.

Just before we were allowed off (the police had to get themselves off their bikes and organised to accompany us across the road before we disembarked), the guide said, 'We have ten minutes at the monument, then we walk to the restaurant for mint tea and cakes, it's just over there'. He indicated a newish, single-storey, rendered building behind us. After his signal, we clambered out. Mum was left sitting on the coach in splendid isolation.

'I don't want to be on my own,' she wailed, 'I'm coming too.' She climbed out last, opening her umbrella in my face and nearly gouging out my eye as she lifted it (the umbrella, not the eye) over her head, which as she was shorter than me by several centimetres, still nearly gouged out my eye, but from a different direction this time.

By now everyone else was at the monument having inscriptions and symbols explained, so a fierce-looking policeman came back for us and, taking Mum's arm, steered us over the road like an over-zealous lollipop man. We stood at the back of the crowd, unable to hear much, but enjoying the view and picking up as much as we could of the information. The rain was pretty heavy by now, but warm and not unpleasant.

After the ten minutes we were shepherded back across the road, Mum walking more and more slowly until Peter reminded her this was a tea stop.

'I want the toilet,' she declared.

'There will be one at the restaurant,' we told her, so once we had arrived, Peter found us a table and I took her to the loo. 'I can't sit there,' she whined on our return, referring to the table.

'Why ever not?' I asked. 'There's a lovely view and it's protected from the rain by the roof.' Peter had picked a table outside; I couldn't see what was wrong.

'I can't sit there,' she repeated, none too quietly. The proprietor heard her.

'What's the matter madam?' he asked.

'I can't sit there, it's in the sun.' There was no sun.

'Where do you want to sit?' he continued, and prepared to pick up the table.

'I don't know.' Mum didn't actually want to sit anywhere, she wanted to make a fuss. Peter saw a large gap and suggested the table went there. The proprietor obligingly moved the table and three chairs and rearranged the cutlery and crockery.

'Some mint tea for you all?' he asked.

'I don't want that stuff, I want orange juice.' Mum was off again.

'You want orange juice, you shall have orange juice,' he said, and off he went, coming back with juice, tea, coffee, chocolate and the famed mint tea on a tray, pouring it out for us all (everyone else was still waiting, and they had all arrived before us). 'Biscuits, cakes or pastries?'

Aha, Mum couldn't resist those, she looked interested at last.

'I'll bring them all,' he said, and he did. Mum chomped her way through most of them. She went to the loo again afterwards and was last back on the coach. We departed the stop and proceeded through the middle of Algiers in the same manner as before. All traffic was stationary, only we moved and the policeman (or it could have been another one) continued to hang out of the lead car door shaking his fist at anyone who even looked as though they were thinking of moving.

We arrived at the church. Huge gates were unlocked and opened for us, and we drove in. The huge gates were locked behind us. Trapped, we entered the church, which was beautiful. We sat and listened to the commentary and collected ourselves after the dash across the city. We boarded again, the gates were unlocked. We drove out. They were relocked.

Our tour of Algiers might have been no frills, but it was certainly many thrills.

'What did you do to get the special treatment?' asked someone as Mum reached her seat. Mum just smirked.

37

MESSAGE IN A BOTTLE

We had checked under the bed to see if the case would fit (it wouldn't) and there was nothing there. We knew there was nothing there. We also had a brilliant steward who cleaned and tidied every day without exception. He would not have allowed anything to be in the wrong place. However, in the middle of the night, when it was rough, there was an almighty thwack as some object fell and landed on the floor. I didn't know what it was, so in case it was important, I woke up Peter, and he was delighted - not. However, he did get out of bed and have a look around. He decided everything was in place and went back to sleep, for a minute or two.

Sleep was not easy when it was rough. It was like having a poltergeist in the room. We were just dropping off to sleep again when CRASH, something else went, so we were out of bed again to shut drawers which were opening and closing to the rhythm of the lurches (they are supposed to lock shut to avoid this, but of course, they don't do as they are told). We placed a chair against them to stop them. We went back to bed again, and quiet reigned. Then, half an hour later, CRASH! A tumbler had fallen, despite being on a non-slip mat, so now there was water everywhere. We put the tumbler (and all the others) on the floor, plus a few bits that might slide. Half an hour later, the contents of the now shut drawers started to slide about inside, up, down, up, down, in time to the rest of the ups and downs. Out of bed again and we put them inside socks or scarves and back in the drawer. Peace at last, then CRASH, a particularly aggressive wave hit us and the whole ship juddered, waking the dead... and so it went on. Then CRASH – oh, it's not a crash, it's the alarm. It had been a long night...

The following morning, an unopened 3-litre bottle of water was rolling back and forth across the cabin floor. Where had it come from? It had not been in our room when we went to bed. We had some 3-litre bottles of water, but they were all present and correct in their special cupboard, on a shelf with a bar across the front of it in order that the bottles would not fall out when it was rough. So where had it come from? We had no idea, so we asked our friends.

Our lovely sister-in-law in Australia had the answer. Someone in Australia did some painstaking research in the 1960s and proved that bottles of water can travel through walls. Yes, honestly, they can! At last, we had the solution.

A few days later, we were on an excursion. We had visited some gardens and were returning to the bus. We sat down ready to go. Two ladies stopped in front of us and started chuntering about someone having taken their bottle of water and left a bag on their seat. They moved the bag with much moaning and proceeded to take up the entire aisle looking for the bottle of water. Log jams developed on both sides, from those climbing on at the front and trying to get to the back, plus those who climbed on in the middle and were trying to get to the front. More chuntering from the two ladies, about people filching things, big bottoms sticking out while bending down to locate the errant bottle.

This went on for some time with very little progress until a passenger pointed out that there was a bottle on another seat, and was it theirs? Yes, they decided, heads nearly knocking together as they straightened up, it was theirs! It was in their bag. Someone must have moved it. It was then suggested that perhaps the bottle was on their original seat, and perhaps they were now in the wrong one. Ah, that was a point, were they in the wrong seat? They all looked the same, maybe they had made a mistake... Yes, they had, that was their seat there, now they had to move back to it. Easier said than done, all the passengers were now on the bus, mostly in the aisle stuck in the log jam. Everyone had to move back out of the way in order that they could swap seats. Lots of toe treading ensued, people falling off steps and things.

'I told you to stay in the same seats,' called the local tour guide, 'I was trying to avoid things like this.'

Trouble was, she was talking to Trekkers; some don't listen and the rest can't hear.

We did wonder if our bottle of water was the one that had jumped from seat to seat on the coach with the ladies with the big bottoms, but if it were, it would have also changed size, changed label and jumped into a carrier bag. I don't think even the Australian of the water bottle experiment would have believed that. Would he?

38

LET OUT OF THE BAG

Morocco on a hot and sunny morning at the fortress. The Trekkers clambered stiffly off the bus, Peter and I taking up the rear. We hadn't really noticed the elderly man waiting at the bottom of the steps. His wrinkled, sunburned face looked up at Peter as he was descending, and his face lit up on seeing him. He grinned widely, revealing one and a half teeth and an awful lot of black gum, as his one black and one white eye reviewed us. He was dressed in the local galabaya, with a head scarf. In one hand he held a sack; the other was behind his back. As Peter reached the bottom step, the hand behind his back was whipped round and held under Peter's nose triumphantly.

'Whaaaa!' is the best rendition of Peter's utterance, as he reversed as quickly as he could up the steps. Unfortunately, as I was close behind, all he managed to do was to send me flying, hitting his head on my front-back pack (I wear it as a front pack, as it's more controllable) while I sat on the top step in an undignified heap.

The old man wheezed, croaked and folded up in mirth, sounding rather like all three of Shakespeare's Scottish witches together. In his hand he held the offending article. A huge snake, clearly disgruntled at having been carted around in a sack all morning, and enjoying the taste of freedom, writhed around the old man's neck, waist and knees, its mouth open, tongue out, still seeking Peter with what was probably great affection, as he had been the reason for the snake's freedom.

It is safe to say Peter was not impressed.

Our next stop was at a Berber village. In case you don't know, the Berbers are the people who ride around on the most amazing horses at 90 miles an hour while shooting great guns that looked for all the world like blunderbusses in the air. The horses (which were probably deafened as foals) have my undying respect.

We sat ourselves down on about six rows of flimsy plastic garden chairs placed under a loggia, facing a racecourse. We were situated at what would normally be the finishing line, right across the course. We realised we were probably better off in the back row, although Mum complained that she couldn't see through the tallest person on the tour who was in front of her. Hearing her not very subtle complaint, this man swapped places with her. She still complained and somehow, she ended up right in the front. Lucky Mum!

Far off in the distance, a cloud of dust rose up. Nearer it came, and the thunder of hooves could be heard. Suddenly they were on top of us. The front row, to a man, cringed back, their chairs sliding from under them, so they finished up in the laps of the people in the second row. Then the blunderbusses went off together, about thirty of them. The second row jumped out of their skins and caused a right melee at the front, with people falling everywhere. Notwithstanding the mayhem, the Berbers went off again to repeat the show while the reverberations from the guns and the echoes from the back of the loggia were still ringing in our ears. We endured this about five times. Those of us not deaf already became so and there must have been a couple of heart attacks, asthma attacks and possibly even a death, but in the maelstrom, they were hardly noticeable.

The next part of our entertainment was an elderly man who beckoned us to leave our chairs and follow him. We were thinking this had got to be better, but it was a bit like the organisation of the coach tickets in the morning. He disappeared into the throng of excited passengers. Peter and I, starting off at the back, didn't get a look in, but intrigued, we joined at the back.

'Closer,' we heard him say. People shuffled forward on the toes of those nearest them. 'Closer still,' we heard him repeat, more shuffling, more cries of 'Ouch,' and 'look where you're standing.' Then there was silence. We held our breath and waited.

Like lightning, a sack emerged from behind him. He emptied it out on the ground in the middle of the tourists. Screams, yells and the position was reversed; the toes of the people behind were trodden on, and they couldn't move back fast enough. Chairs and people scattered to the four winds. Amid this, about eight snakes were writhing on the ground to the delight of the old man and the horror of our shipmates. Like seasoned pros, I said, 'Oh, that trick again, we've seen it before.'

With great skill, he deftly caught several of the snakes by their tails and replaced them in his sack. Bedlam continued for several minutes, then began to die down. The old man began hunting between chairs and people,

'Three missing,' he declared.

Bedlam again. People were now standing on the plastic chairs, which were not designed for that kind of use. They wobbled, broke and fell over, and just a handful remained intact.

'Three missing,' he repeated, cackling away to himself. He looked in the sack, rummaged around a bit and continued, 'My mistake, my mistake.'

There was a collective sigh of relief that he had found them. But no...

'Four missing, four missing,' he shouted with delight.

39

WATCHING THE BIRDIE – AND NEARLY MISSING THE BOAT

Quite a place, Tasmania. There is a Cadbury's factory in Hobart, originally set up to produce drinking chocolate to wean people off alcohol (as if) and opium poppies grow for the pharmaceutical industry. An idea for the future might be to combine the poppies and chocolate to give it that extra zing. I'm amazed an enterprising person hasn't been to Dragons' Den to suggest it.

We visited an animal sanctuary while in Tasmania and I completely fell for a sulphur-crested cockatoo aged 98 and named Bert; I chatted to him and he came right up to me on the wires of his cage. While I was chatting (I'm obviously fluent in Birdish), Bert kept completely still, so lots of people managed to take good photographs of him. His story, as with most animals at sanctuaries, was sad; he had been a pet and very badly treated, so he didn't trust humans and was very nervous.

Suddenly, one of the foreigners in our party started shouting at someone else in his own language, waving his camera about and nearly hitting me. He got so close, I had to jump back. Poor neurotic Bert took off and went to the bottom of his cage and stayed there throughout our visit, which was two hours long. Now no one could photograph him. A keeper tried to feed him grapes, but he wasn't having any of it; the shouting had completely upset him.

We were asked to return to the coach by 1.15, and of the 28 of us, 27 did so. The person missing had been sitting directly in front of us. We waited so long that the local guide, the Beeline escort and another passenger who knew our absentee went off in different directions to try and find him. Eventually, he sauntered back at 1.40, not in the least sorry. He got some stick; there were three men sitting near him and they all had a go. He totally ignored them.

We then had to wait for everyone else to return (the person who knew him was not at all happy to have to go off looking for him and told him so in no uncertain terms). The tour guide said we were now returning for lunch on board and one person commented that there wouldn't be any left by the time we got back. The tour guide then suggested we should go back into Hobart for the afternoon, and another person said there wouldn't be time for that either now. The miscreant still ignored the comments, but you can probably guess who it was. Yes, Bert's tormentor.

We were on several later tours with the same man and something must have stuck, as he wasn't late again.

40

PETER DANCES THE HORNPIPE

The charming John Carter, famous for introducing a popular holiday programme on television, was with us. He gave a talk, advising us to avoid the four Fs while on holiday, and no, he wasn't swearing. Two of them were folklore shows and food, the others escape me. Too late, Mum, Peter and I had already signed up for the St Petersburg folklore show that evening, having been to the ballet the last time we were in Russia. The theatre we attended was, in true Russian style, beautiful, and the first half of the show riveting; gorgeous costumes, phenomenal music, lovely singing voices and breath-taking dances. What on earth was the matter with a folklore show?

At the interval, we were to have champagne and nibbles. Being placed right in the middle of a line about ten rows back, and with all the other people about three decades older than we were and rather slow at the best of times, it took us some time to leave the auditorium and emerge into the hall where the refreshments were to be served.

Mum was peeved. 'I want to go to the toilet. When we come back, there won't be anything left.'

She wanted to visit the lavatory first, so we trekked down 50 stairs to the basement where the only washrooms were (so sensible, when all the business was done on the top floors) and then up again rather more slowly.

'I'll never get anything to eat at this rate, it will all be gone by the time we get there.'

She had moaned when Peter picked the seats, but he wanted us to be in the centre. Less chance of us being picked for anything there, and she was doing it again now.

Arriving last and at last, in the hall, all the party were standing around at one side, while waiters filled a long trestle table on the other side with food. Taking no chances, having experienced cruise parties before, they had cordoned off the table with little portable posts and a thick cord looped all the way along, in the front of the table in order that they could get out of the firing line when the refreshments were open and the gannets descended. Plates were piled at one end, and there was still an expanse of tablecloth to be covered at the other.

Mum wasn't having any of this waiting around lark. She walked straight up to the pile of plates, took one and helped herself, tripping and falling across the barrier to do so.

'Mum!' Peter remonstrated, replacing two of the little posts which had been on their sides. 'The refreshments aren't ready yet, wait, come over here.'

'What?' asked Mum, helping herself to a couple of sandwiches.

'It isn't ready yet, look, everyone else is still waiting.'

'What for? We'll be going back in soon.'

'They haven't taken away the barrier yet, they can make the interval as long as they like, there's only us.'

She looked around at us, defiant, as we stood there horrified. Then she noticed we were alone in the middle of the room, and tried to put back the sandwiches. I caught her wrist.

'Leave them on your plate, come over here, wait with the others,' I said. By this time, 'the others' were looking on in delighted fascination. Mum was impossible to embarrass.

'Where's the champagne then?' Mum asked. Hearing the tinkle of glassware behind her, she turned. 'About time too,' she grumbled, but we did stop her taking a glass from one of the waiters, who was now placing a tray of full glasses on the table. We moved her away, towards the crowd the other side of the room, trying to be anonymous.

As the table setting was complete, so the cordon was cleared away from the front. Instantly, the crowd converged on it and the tea party started. The crowd coming towards us met the three of us making our way towards them. They, being rather larger than we were, had the better of us. Sandwiches went one way, many trodden underfoot into the carpet, as Mum went another. Undaunted, she turned back to the table and helped herself to more of the same, and at the end of the interval she walked back with us to the auditorium with one damp arm and tomato down the front of her dress, chirpy at having had her money's worth.

Peter and I settled back in our seats, grateful for anonymity, as a young lady came onto the stage. She looked around, spied Peter and beckoned to him. Oh no, this was just what we had wanted to avoid by tucking ourselves right in the middle of the audience. Peter had two left feet, no sense of rhythm and did not like the limelight. We both shook our heads vigorously. She put her head on one side, mouthed 'Please,' and beckoned again. We shook our heads again, so she came down from the stage, worked her way to our row and began squeezing herself along to get to Peter. She must have been watching for the youngest person there and she was determined she would have him.

As she approached us, I said, 'He can't dance and

he has no sense of rhythm, please choose someone else'. She put her head on one side again, said 'please' and put her hands together as though she was praying. Several people round us, safe in the knowledge that if Peter joined in, they wouldn't have to, shouted encouragement. In the end, we couldn't refuse. Peter went up on stage while I sat, dreading what was to come, and the people round me nudged, winked and giggled.

The Russians started a folk dance while Peter and the young lady watched. The dance went on for one turn, stopped and made way for this ill matched pair to join them. Peter was brilliant! He was foot perfect, on time and dancing with a straight back and a smile, looked confident and professional. Where had he learned how to do it?

At the end, the applause was deafening; roars, whistles (the appreciative sort) and cheers erupted as Peter was accompanied back to his seat. He even had a standing ovation from some, unless they were standing because didn't actually have seats themselves. He was patted on his back as he threaded his way towards me,

'You shouldn't hide his light under a bushel,' the chap the other side of Peter said to me. 'He was brilliant, and it was videoed too.' I had no idea it was being videoed. 'Oh, yes,' he continued, 'they were videoing at the interval too, between Peter and his mother, it's been a good night.' He laughed.

I'm always proud of Peter, but that was a shining moment. Congratulating him, I asked him how he had done it.

He smiled. 'I remembered what John Carter said, all folklore dances are the same, so I did the Gay Gordons.'

Lo and behold, the videos were on sale in the foyer at the end, but we didn't buy one. Sometimes, I regret it.

41

COMING FULL CIRCLE

We made some new Australian friends on a North African cruise and spent an interesting evening in Tripoli with them. At the end of the cruise we exchanged addresses and they offered to show us round Sydney if we ever went there.

A few years later we were on our Canadian cruise, which took us to St John's, Newfoundland. We saw a small dark blue and rust-coloured ship in the harbour, which didn't look as though it was going anywhere. In fact it looked a pretty awful rust bucket, which was a shame as her lines were beautiful.

We were told the following story about her. In 2011, a Russian cruise liner visited St John's. The port authorities inspected her and failed her. Having done that, they had to impound her. The Russians offered an inducement of 40,000 Canadian dollars to pass her and let her continue her cruise, but the Canadians were not to be moved. The crew and passengers were stranded, so the locals had a whip round to send them all back to Russia. Two months before we arrived, the port authorities tried to start the engines, to move her, but they were in such a bad state, they had to be shut down — and so did the town and the harbour. There was so much smoke, people thought there had been a terrorist attack.

The ship was roughly 10,000 tons (a midget by today's standards) and the Canadians were looking for buyers. We were offered the ship for one Canadian dollar, but we didn't buy it; we offered it to our friends when we arrived home, we even had a dollar we offered to lend them at very little interest, but they showed very little interest too. We left St John's with the sad ship still sitting in the harbour.

Six months later, we were in Sydney with our friends. Peter phoned them from the ship; we could see them waiting for us on the dockside about 100 metres away, but the reception in the poor weather suffered, and the conversation went something like this 'ha... are you... we... late... can you he...? Din... yes... can't... bye!'

They took us to The Rocks, an area of Sydney which had been notoriously slummy and dangerous in days past, named after the oldest sandstone rock in the world, which the convicts used to work and use for building. We visited a museum in Susannah Place which told some of the history of the area. A terrace of four houses and a grocer's shop, it was built in 1844 and named after a family member. The family who built it were Irish Protestant immigrants who lived in one house and rented the others. Over 100 families lived in the terrace, and by following them up, the curator had compiled a surprisingly full history of the road. It was a wonderful museum, the highlight of our time in Sydney (and that included the Opera House).

We chatted to the Russian curator, and our friends told him we were on a cruise. His reply was that he had only ever been on one cruise, just last year, which he then described. It sounded somehow familiar as he went on to say they had had to abandon their ship in St John's, Newfoundland. We asked the name of the ship, knowing that we knew, but just checking. We were able to confirm it was still there and that he could buy it for a Canadian dollar if he wanted to, but he was as reluctant as everyone else to buy it.

Small world, isn't it?

42

PICKY EATERS

The choice for lunch was between chicken and fish. It was our second day in Sydney and we were visiting the Blue Mountains. It was simple really, the local guide wanted us to do a tally. She sent a piece of paper off round the coach with two columns, headed 'chicken' on one side and 'fish' on the other. We were to make a stroke under our preference and every fifth stroke was to be diagonally through the other four. Did we know what she meant, were we familiar with tallying? Yes and yes.

So, the paper came round. Could people actually do it? No, of course not. Peter and I were almost the last to add our strokes to the list and it was a complete mess. Apart from anything else, the number of strokes was not the same as the number of people on the bus; it was about three times as large. I think some passengers had put four strokes with a diagonal line for one lunch. I also wondered how many passengers would change their minds at the last minute. Still, no doubt we would get something and we wouldn't go hungry. Even if we ate nothing, the standard of food on board was so good we would not suffer.

We arrived at the lunch stop. I had chosen chicken. Bad choice, it was about a millimetre thick, breaded and overcooked. It would have done well on my shoe. The vegetables had puréed themselves and sat in an unattractive puddle of water around the congealing gravy. I wasn't sure if the potatoes were boiled or mashed, as they weren't quite either. Peter's grey fish didn't look a great alternative either. The apple pie was all pie and no apple and the custard was cold. Apart from that, it was wonderful.

When we arrived back on the coach, the local guide asked us if we had enjoyed our lunch. The answer was a resounding 'no'. She then proceeded to tell us we were difficult to please and picky to boot. So tactful. She then sat sulking, saying nothing while we were driven to the forest excursion, our next venue.

We arrived at our stop in the Blue Mountains and she explained that the train we were supposed to ride on was out of order, and the pathway we were supposed to walk along was closed. The only transport open was a cable car, so she suggested we should go for a ride on that, get off it and get straight back on again to come back. We went off in the cable car, found the path open, had a delightful walk in the forest and came back when we wanted to.

There was silence on the way back, until she started telling us the most unfunny jokes you have ever heard. These were either ignored because people were asleep or because they had given up the will to live. She then asked why we had lost our sense of humour - she was lucky no one told her.

Lastly, it was our fault the traffic lights were all red, because we were not thinking green.

I wonder if she is still in the same job?

43

JUST ORDINARY

Mum's life was dominated by her watch. Every meal and every snack was taken at a particular time. On one occasion she asked me if I thought she had enough time to do the ironing before lunch. My reply was, 'If you need to do the ironing, do it and get lunch afterwards, or I'll do it for you while you prepare lunch.'

She thought a moment, and replied 'I don't have time.'

When we were out, if Mum looked at her watch before 11 am, she made no comment. At 11, she would say, I'm thirsty, I need to stop for a coffee.' If it was after 11, it would be, 'I'm absolutely parched, I've got to have a coffee.'

We tried to intercept this by identifying a coffee spot before 11, but our ideas on coffee shops were different. Mum still lived in the 1950s, an era when life was perfect, the weather was perfect, the shops in the High Street sold everything she needed and time stood still. We remembered rationing, limited ranges of food and clothing in stores, chilblains, fogged-up windows and continuous rain. Well, not quite continuous, it stopped in the winter for a bit of yellow London smog, some snow and occasionally we saw the sun, but do you remember anyone with a suntan in the 1950s? If you do, they must have been abroad. Mum thought the sun shone every day and she loved her cafés with Formica tables or checked tablecloths, plastic-seated chairs and the lingering smell of cigarettes and all-day breakfast. We preferred the trademarked shops.

On this particular day, we had been to the shops, as we were 'doing our own thing' and not going on an excursion. Mum had bought a cardigan. Knitwear shops come in three divisions; the downmarket shops kind of fold your knitwear and put it in a plastic carrier bag, the middling ones fold it, unwrapped, and put it in a paper carrier, with rope or paper handles. The very best wrap it in tissue paper sealed with a circular spot of sticky tape, put it in a paper carrier with some perfumed beads and close the top with another circular piece of sticky tape and a decorative ribbon tied in a bow. Mum had been to a middling store and I was carrying the bag for her, which, as it was paper, stood slightly open.

We arrived at a trademarked coffee shop just before 11, and Peter took a tray and ordered for the two of us; two small skinny cappuccinos and two almond croissants. Mum always liked to do her own ordering and have her own tray. She asked for an ordinary coffee. The waitress, who was foreign, asked her again and Mum said, 'I want an ordinary coffee.'

'What size?' asked the girl.

'Just ordinary,' replied Mum.

The girl looked puzzled.

'Small, medium or large, Mum?' Peter put in.

'Just ordinary,' persisted Mum.

'A small Americano,' Peter translated.

'I want hot milk,' demanded Mum, as the girl poured some cold milk into a jug. The girl continued pouring. We didn't say anything. We just watched. Mum huffed and puffed.

'I want a cake,' continued Mum, 'one of those,' indicating the Danish pastries. The girl understood that and collected some tongs as another person made the coffee,

'Which one?' she asked.

'The yellow one,' said Mum.

The girl indicated an apricot pastry. 'This one?'

'No.'

The only other yellow one was custard, (as there were raspberry jam and cinnamon swirl, red and brown respectively), so I stepped in fairly confidently and suggested the custard pastry. Mum was just about to say 'no' when she realised it was the only other yellow one and had to agree it was what she wanted. The girl placed it on a plate, which she handed to Mum.

'I want a knife,' said Mum.

'Cutlery, crockery and condiments are all behind you.' The girl pointed over my shoulder. Mum turned to look. As she did so, she tipped the plate and the Danish pastry slid off it, depositing itself neatly in the carrier bag, the custard side nestling up to the side of her cardigan – but neither of us noticed this. Mum turned back to put the plate on her tray and saw, with amazement, that it was empty. We looked for the pastry, but couldn't find it anywhere. Eventually, after a wail or two of 'where's my cake? It's gone, who took it?' the girl gave her another.

We went to a table where Mum complained that her coffee was cold, so Peter took the cold milk and asked for some hot, which he brought back. The coffee was now too hot, the cup too heavy and the volume too much. We drank up and left.

Arriving back, I gave Mum her carrier bag. She didn't touch the cardigan for about three days. Then we heard all about it, and so did everyone else on the table.

Mum wanted her hair done. The hairdresser was located in the bowels of the ship and Mum wanted me to go with her to make an appointment, just in case she got lost. We arrived just after another lady who was making two appointments. Mum leaned on me while she waited, impatiently, for the receptionist to be ready. After waiting for a minute or two, the receptionist was available.

'How can I help you?' she asked.

'I want my hair done on Wednesday morning,' was the reply.

'Shampoo?' asked the receptionist.

'Yes,' said Mum.

'Shampoo and set, or blow dry?'

'Just ordinary,' replied Mum.

'Is that a set or a blow dry?'

'Just ordinary.'

'Ordinary what?' asked the girl.

'Just ordinary.' The girl was being very good; she didn't show any impatience or anything, she must have been used to it, but I was wondering how long Mum could keep it up.

'Just an ordinary shampoo and set,' I supplied.

'Yes,' said Mum, 'Just ordinary.'

44

DRAGONS

We had landed on an island in the South Pacific. The port lecturer had told us that under no circumstances were we to walk along the sand. It was written in our daily newspaper too. The sand is home to a very tiny mosquito-like creature. Clothing is no barrier to it and it bites and can then burrow into your skin, where it usually leaves infections. It's called, appropriately, the no-no fly. There is also a tree here which bears gigantic fruit like strawberries which, if you make it into a drink, cures everything. It's called the no-ni tree. The language here has no imagination about it at all. Don't get the tree mixed up with the flies, whatever you do.

So, we went for a stroll along the promenade, and what do you know, there was a group of passengers walking along the beach, kicking up the sand as they went.

Later we cruised to Indonesia and Komodo island. I thought I knew what I was in for when we booked. These huge lizards are the largest in the world. The received wisdom currently states that these can reach a length of three metres and that the largest ever was just over this. Maybe they stop at this length in zoos, but the alpha male and his harem we saw appeared far larger that morning. Komodo dragons are protected, as there are only about 4,000 of them in the wild, and half live on Komodo itself. I foolishly thought we would be walking behind wire netting to glimpse a sight of them in the distance through binoculars. Not so. These animals are as fast as crocodiles; they can outrun humans, as they can run as fast as 20 kph in heat and humidity. They like water and can dive up to 4.5 metres, although they can only swim for 500 metres before they have to stop. They can smell one drop of blood from several miles and enjoy the flavour of human flesh. This last point clearly indicates that no one has actually gone up to a Komodo dragon and said, 'Come along Cuddles, just stay still a moment with your mouth shut while I use my tape measure to see just how long you are from your nose to the tip of your tail'.

Believe me, our dragons were huge. Their tails

were long enough and strong enough to sweep a small group of people off their feet with one swish.

The *Daily Times* instructions were more or less as follows. We were to go on the island only as part of the cruise line party; we could not wander off on our own. We were allowed on the island only if we had no wounds and were not menstruating, and we were not to wear red or flesh-coloured clothes. We had to wear closed in, comfortable shoes. We were to stay with our two park rangers, who would be armed with sticks.

We then found out that two rangers had been eaten as they were sleeping, a couple of weeks before we went; they had not shut their door properly. A young boy from the village (there is just one village on Komodo), had been eaten the week before when he had been playing in the trees. If you are bitten, we were told, the saliva is so poisonous from bacteria that you die within hours and there is no antidote, although very recent research has indicated that they may inject venom and this is what kills so effectively. Komodo dragons are cold blooded, so they don't use any more energy that they have to; they bite their prey, sit back and watch it die. I was beginning to wish we were somewhere else.

Malaria mosquitoes are not around during the day in Komodo, but others, carrying other deadly infections, are, so we had to be protected from them too – oh, and the sun of course, so hats and sunscreen were necessary.

Komodo is a very tiny island. Flores, next door, is larger, and the rangers who do not actually live on Komodo mostly come from there. They must breathe a sigh of relief each time they go back!

We approached the island by tender, and guess what? On the boat was a woman wearing a huge red sunhat and a top covered with a red poppy pattern. Honestly, we couldn't believe it, after all we had been told. There was quite a lot of muttering, but no one said anything to her. Thank goodness she wasn't in our group. (The tender held about eighty, we were split into groups of twenty).

Disembarking from the tender was fun. The tide was high and there was a barrier round the landing stage that we had to get under to get off the boat. In addition to climbing four steps within the boat itself, with the boat bobbing about, avoiding the roof of the tender and the barrier, which were both at about waist height once you reached the fourth step up, this was difficult. We then had to negotiate two steps down onto the rather rickety jetty. GCSE limbo dancing would have come in so handy.

Peter and I made it reasonably easily, jumping like gazelles, but not so some others. We were well through the cruise by now, so some passengers had put on rather a lot of weight, and they were old, so imagine, if you can, a 20-stone 80-year-old man who usually uses a stick to get around trying to limbo off the tender. He was already melting in the heat and humidity of the morning, and was getting completely stuck as he didn't fold in the middle. His friends were shouting encouragement as they pushed from behind, while he was being pulled from the outside by helpful staff, trying to keep straight faces. We saw some interesting angles on big bottoms.

The rangers, all tall slim and fit with not a drop of sweat between them, lined themselves up to greet us, or maybe it was just to watch the antics. Anyway, they had front row seats as they watched this totally undignified landing of people they were supposed to keep safe from the animals. Christmas pantomimes came to mind. The rangers didn't laugh too much, although some seemed to have salt in their eyes, as they had to keep wiping them. They seemed to be doing demonstrations of what to do, as they kept folding themselves double, half squatting down, holding their sides, rocking backwards and forwards and emitting strange groans and gasps. We noticed no ranger made eye contact with any other ranger; it must be some tradition.

We were greeted by our particular guide and two rangers. We knew the rangers only had sticks, but they were a bit pathetic (the sticks, not the rangers). About two metres in length with a girth slightly more than that of my thumb, these sticks were Y shaped. At the top, where they bifurcated, the two branches were about twenty centimetres long. Not very impressive to keep away tons of ferocious and deadly animal.

We set off on our walk, the guide and a ranger at the front and another ranger at the back. We were lucky, as we were the second group to go and it was only 8 am. Although it was already hot, the lizards were not likely to be very lively yet.

We walked along a small path through the jungle, no barbed wire, no little fences, nothing between us and... well, anything. We were told in passing that as lizards are quite capable of being cannibals, the young ones live up in the trees and could drop on us at any time, rather like Sir Arthur Conan Doyle's "Lost World", really. No, the guide didn't know how old or big they grew before their saliva became venomous, but we should watch out. Even a baby Komodo falling on us was not a good thing. Great. We needed eyes everywhere.

As we approached a clearing, we saw three huge male lizards in front of us. All were at least ten feet long, and they looked at us with complete boredom. Unfortunately, they can change mood in a flash, and if they had, we were only three or four metres from them, with no protection except the sticks, and nowhere to go. We took photos, just to prove we had seen them, and one elderly lady on her own asked someone else to take her picture for her. A chap took her camera, but he couldn't get her in with the lizards in the background as they were too close, so he asked her to squat down. She did this, he took the photo and then she couldn't get up again. It took about three people to pull her up, but in the end they managed. The lizards missed a treat there, as they would have had plenty of time to pounce.

We walked back to the jetty, keeping to the paths as we had been told. We definitely felt some relief to be out of the domain of the dragons. One woman came back along the sand, which wasn't recommended. As she walked some people on the jetty waved to her, she waved back, they waved more furiously and shouted to her, she continued to wave and to walk. Only then did she realise that there was a young lizard running after her. Suddenly, she was off like Usain Bolt and just reached the jetty in time. It was exciting in retrospect, and she looked very funny trotting along with a lizard, looking rather like a sausage dog, running along behind her. But, as I said, it is only funny in retrospect.

One group had a really bad time. They went later in the morning when the lizards were feeling frisky and just a bit fed up with being gawped at by yet another lot of humans. As the guide was explaining about the trees, one of his group heard a sound behind her, and when she turned round, there was a dragon. A ranger had been alerted by the sound at the same time and came to the rescue with his stick just in time. Unfortunately the dragon wouldn't take no for an answer and kept coming back. We did wonder if someone in the group was either wearing the wrong colour or was bleeding, as the animal was so persistent. Altogether, a morning to remember.

During the afternoon, the children from the village came out to the ship in little dugout canoes. They were asking us for money, the idea being that we put change in an empty water bottle which would float, throw it to them and they would either catch it or row to it. Some people did, though many more threw fruit, which also floated. The boys were so quick, some diving off the canoe and swimming to the fruit to claim it and not share it. They were like little dolphins, they were so good in the water.

We were watching with another passenger as she threw an apple, two oranges and a banana to them. As she was throwing, a chap came up, pulled her by her shoulder and said, in a venomous voice, 'Don't you dare do that! It is totally against maritime law, you should never throw anything over the side, and I am going to complain to a senior member of the crew.' He stormed off. We were horrified. We watched him go up to a member of the crew, who shook his head and did an imitation of the breast stroke. He appeared to be saying that we weren't throwing rubbish, but giving to the boys, who were swimming after whatever was thrown. A few minutes later, the captain came on the speaker and asked that the fruit throwing should stop now as we were about to move and it would then be dangerous for the little boys.

The little boys were most disappointed (they could hear, and understood the English) and hung around as we moved, trying to keep up with us and waving at the same time, but steering well out to the side of us. Gradually they fell back and we saw them no more.

There's always one.

45

KITTED OUT - OR NOT

We should have known we were in for it when Mum asked us to go with her to buy some new evening dresses for the next cruise.

We visited a House of Fraser store. Peter and I were sure they would have something for Mum, who was about 82 at the time. They had so many franchise stores for the young, the more mature, the tall and the petite that they were bound to have something, weren't they? We had gone out especially with her.

When we arrived at the store, she changed her mind. 'I've decided I don't want to buy anything now after all,' she announced.

'We're here now,' said Peter. 'We are at least going to see what there is.'

That was when I thought there might be trouble. We entered the store and walked to the escalator; the ladies' clothing was all upstairs. We passed a long dress and jacket.

'What do you think of this?' I asked.

'I don't want a jacket with it,' she said, and walked on.

Peter found a lace top and skirt in lilac. 'How about this?' he asked.

'I want a dress, not a skirt and top!' She was getting louder.

I found a rail of evening dresses. 'There might be something here,' I called. 'These are very attractive.'

'I can't wear those, they haven't got sleeves,' she said, louder still. She had now attracted the attention of an assistant, who came over to see what the fuss was about.

'Can I help?' she asked.

'Yes,' I said.

'No,' said Mum.

'My mother-in-law is looking for evening dresses, can you help her please?' I pleaded. 'We aren't having much luck.'

'You haven't got any dresses here,' Mum snapped, 'none at all.'

'Oh, but we have, lots,' answered the assistant. She

was right, they had hundreds, and it was true that some were clearly not suitable, but lots were.

'I am sure we can find you a dress you like. What exactly do you want?' she went on.

'A dress for me,' Mum replied, unhelpfully.

The assistant walked over to one of the franchises for the petite and picked out two long dresses with sleeves and without jackets.

'How about something like this?' she showed them to Mum,

'I don't think they're what I want at all, I don't like the colour.'

'They look better on, and they come in different colours, why don't you try them?'

'I don't want to try them.'

'Well, you won't buy anything if you don't try anything on.' The assistant was just a shade sharp now.

'Just try them,' Peter and I begged. She took the dresses ungraciously and disappeared with them. A few minutes later, she was back.

'They look awful,' she announced. 'I want a cup of tea, it's tea time.'

Mum has never asked us to go shopping for dresses again and in fact, she wore the same dresses for the formal nights from then on until and including her last cruise about six years later.

46

BATTLE OF THE SOUTH PACIFIC

Once again, we were in the South Pacific. We docked at the local container port as usual, the *Beeline Bounty* being small enough to fit into it nice and snugly. We didn't notice immediately that there were no little stalls of local goodies for sale. There also didn't appear to be any taxis in view. We usually had to run the gauntlet of dozens of taxi drivers asking us if we wanted to hire them every time we disembarked, even when it was clear we were on a tour. What we did see was a motley collection of buses, coaches and minibuses.

Out behind us, a much bigger ship came in after us, and was now anchored at sea, tendering off its passengers to a spot on the dockside half a kilometre or so away from us.

We departed for our tour of the island. We visited the royal palace, watched some dancing with men in grass skirts and were serenaded by school children. The girls were wearing the box pleated gym slips that were worn until about the 1950s in the UK. We then went off to the beach and watched pigs paddling around to find fish (no, they weren't flying, this is all true). We ended up at a museum, and as we hadn't been given a return time on the bus, the Beeline escort suggested we should just take as much time as it takes. Very South Pacific, very relaxed. Our tour had been a bit chaotic; no one was quite ready for us, no one quite knew what to say to us, but we all had fun.

On the way back, our driver kindly stopped to point out flying foxes in the trees. This was a great treat as we had never seen any bats anywhere near approaching their size - they were enormous. Later on the journey, we passed the landing place of the other ship's tenders. Local stalls were set out, taxis were waiting and a brass band was playing. Clearly, this ship was more welcome on the island than ours.

Returning to our ship, we detected quite an atmosphere of anger and unrest. Over lunch, we found out what it was all about. The owner of the cruise line was actually on our cruise with his family, and they had all sat at the table next to ours, but the table was empty now.

The story came out bit by bit. It transpired that the larger ship out to sea had not ordered enough coaches for its passengers, so it had bribed the police, saying that if the police would order our coaches to turn round, their cruise line would pay more than our cruise line had paid and use the coaches instead. The police agreed and the coaches, buses or minibuses which had not left our dock were boarded by the police and everyone inside was ordered off. The local guides were not all ready to comply however, and told some of the coaches full of passengers to stay put, saying that if they did that, the excursion would have to go ahead. So we had a situation where some excursions were unaffected, some were going off very late because the passengers refused to get off their transport, and some people were being turned off the coaches and going nowhere.

At dinner in the evening, one person on our table had been out on an all-day excursion during which they had visited a restaurant for lunch. The passengers from the other ship had gatecrashed the restaurant, sat themselves down at several tables and demanded food. The restaurant had refused to serve some, turning them out, so our guests did have lunch, but one table from the other ship had remained because they had told the proprietor they were from our ship. When he had been put right, and as their cruise line was not paying for them, the restaurateur asked for payment at the end, and made out a bill. They refused to pay it. Doors were locked, our passengers were escorted out and the last our table mates knew, the other passengers were locked in the restaurant alone until they paid their bill.

At dinner, our cruise line owner was present, and by then we had all had a letter in our cabins to let us know how angry he was. He told us his cruise line would never call at that island again, and he was taking the other cruise line to court as soon as we arrived in a suitable country to do this. Meanwhile, we would all have our money back for our excursions, whether they had gone ahead or not. You really couldn't say fairer than that.

As we left that evening, the brass band arrived and played us out. Were they trying to ingratiate themselves to us? We will never know.

The following day, we were chatting to the guest relations officer in her office, which was next to the excursions office. She went out to find some paperwork for us and we heard a conversation going on at the excursions desk.

'How can I help you?'

'Excuse me, but you know everyone had their money refunded for their trips yesterday?'

'Yes.'

'Well, we didn't go out on a trip, but if we had

known about getting your money back, we would have, so can we have some money back anyway?'

The answer was an unsurprising, 'No, I'm sorry, you can't'.

'But why not?'

I couldn't believe my ears. I checked with Peter that I wasn't hearing things; I wasn't. When Janet came back with her paperwork, I told her what we had heard.

'Oh yes,' she said, shaking her head slightly, 'there has been a steady stream of them all morning asking the same thing. They won't get anything of course, but they always try.'

There's no pleasing some people.

Two years later we met the captain of the *Beeline Bounty* when we were in the Baltic and asked him what had transpired after the above debacle. He told us that at last all was well between the cruise companies and that Beeline would now be going back to the island.

47

GETTING CRAFTY

We were having a masked ball on one cruise, and we had all been given small masks to decorate in black and white. During the afternoon, the crafts room would be opened and we could help ourselves to paintbrushes and glue, sequins, beads, lace and feathers and anything else that took our fancy. I was looking forward to it and expected Mum to ask if I would take hers with me to decorate both. I would have been happy to do it (assuming she asked reasonably nicely). I was surprised then when she decided to come with me and complete her own.

When we arrived in the craft room there were

about twenty of us altogether, and Mum and I found places together at a table for about eight. Mum kept my place beside her as I helped the people moving boxes and arranging all the exciting bits and pieces to use on all the tables reasonably fairly. Some tables had more than others of some components and the idea was that if we couldn't find what we wanted at our own table, we were free to wander, but hopefully not too many would be wandering at once.

There was a boxful of glue brushes, and among them, one tiny paintbrush. I had my eye on it for Mum.

'Lilian ought to have that one,' someone told me, 'It'll be easier for her.' I was grateful and said so. Most people knew Mum, knew she had difficulties and knew she was difficult. You couldn't keep Mum quiet on a cruise.

Settling down at the tables, there was a lull as we all decided what we wanted, sharing out between us the beads and sequins, and trying not to breathe too hard as it sent them all off the table onto the floor. We had learned that by bitter experience. We had to remember not to laugh too hard either, and in so doing found everything amusing and couldn't stop laughing.

We got to work with the beads and feathers which had survived the giggles. Mum dabbed her tiny brush into the glue, took it out without wiping it on the lip of the top of the glue pot and dripped a huge splodge onto her mask, far too much to be useful.

'Oh, I can't do this, you'll have to do it for me,' she

wailed. She pushed the mask away, put down the brush and sat back.

'Can't you see Rose is busy?' I heard, 'You'll never get it done if you don't try. Give it a go, you never know what you can do till you've tried.' Wow, someone was standing up to her.

'When I have finished mine, I'll see what I can do for you,' I said to Mum, smiling at the lady opposite who had put her in her place. 'Meanwhile, do what the lady says, and give it a go.'

If looks could kill, Mum would have been alone among the dead, but she pulled the mask towards her and I dabbed at her glue spot with a tissue, suggesting she should try arranging some sequins on it. To be fair, she tried, but she now had glue on her finger, and as she pressed the sequin to the mask, it determinedly stayed there. She huffed, puffed and wailed, 'Oh, I can't do this,' and looked round for effect. Usually, it was difficult to make eye contact with Mum, but she wanted something now, and she was looking at someone —anyone – to give her a hand. Nobody was obliging.

'Just wait,' I said. I couldn't bear the silence, and besides, she was my mother-in-law. 'Draw round the outline in black while you wait,' I suggested. She picked up a black pen and started drawing, quietly.

The table continued to work, we chatted a bit, feathers flew around if we breathed too hard, sequins stuck everywhere but in the correct place, and black pens decided to run out at the most inconvenient time; the usual sorts of things that happen when you do craft with a group. It was fun, and bit by bit, the masks took shape. We all took it in turns to go on sequin watch on the table, each with a tiny dab of glue on a finger going round the floor, gathering as many sequins and beads as we had lost and replacing them on the table. I think nearly all of us hit our heads on something while we were scrabbling around on the floor. The feathers were the worst; they stuck to the floor, our fingers and the table, anywhere but on the masks, and in the end they looked bedraggled and sparse. Many feathers were unusable after they'd had the craft room treatment, and our fingers had little bits of feather stuck to them which we couldn't get off.

Mum sat waiting for me, doodling now on some paper. Some people finished and left, others were taking much longer, and one person took pity on Mum and offered to help, then another offered. They both put beads and lace on her mask, while Mum tried cutting the lace into small pieces for them.

I finished my mask and asked Mum what else she wanted on hers. She wasn't sure, but between us we managed a halfway decent mask for her; she seemed pleased. I left her with both masks while they dried, and began to help clear away. We weren't quite the last, and time was getting on.

'You are so lucky,' I heard a voice say, 'I wouldn't go on a cruise with my mother-in-law if you paid me all the tea in China.' It was the lady opposite, who was still clearing up. Mum said nothing. We departed in silence.

Mum's mask had now been created by several of us, but when it came to the masked ball, she wasn't wearing it.

'Where's your mask?' Peter asked.

'The elastic broke, so I can't wear it,' replied Mum.

48

INANIMATE OBJECTS

If the people and the weather don't get to you on a cruise, the inanimate objects will. Take our bathroom on one Atlantic cruise. It was a beautiful bathroom with his and hers basins, lots of beautiful toiletries, pure thick, fluffy, Egyptian cotton towels changed every time we used them, a bath and a shower... well, not exactly a shower, more a hose from the bath and without a mixer tap. Nor was there a nice little dial on the wall for the thermostat. No, just the bath taps. In the off position, the blue and red blobs on the taps had no relation to each other; they didn't line up nicely to show you they were off, nor were they at right angles to each other, they were just sort of random. The shower was completely pathetic; if you had to fill a bath using it, it would take you all day.

I tried the shower before Peter. I took the shower head off the hook and tried to have a shower at a comfortable temperature. Easier said than done. In order to work it, there was a tiny knob the size of a small shirt button that had to be pressed in on the back of the hot tap. It was positioned so that you had to press really hard (there was a similar knob on the cold tap which also pushed in, but appeared to do nothing). Once pressed in, the hot tap had to be turned the opposite way to normal (turn it the normal way and the knob sprang out and you filled the bath – well, you didn't fill it, you kind of trickled it) while the cold went in the opposite direction, or the normal way. Trying to strike a balance between the two for the temperature was fraught, as you had to hold the hose between your knees to free both hands for fiddling with the hot and cold taps. When you reached the right temperature, the hose could go back on the hook, but woe betide you if you knocked the hose; one wrong move, and it became an angry snake. The head would turn and spray everything but you – the bathroom, the floor, the door, the mirror, the bathmat, the lot. Even once you started to shower with the head in the right place, the challenges continued, as the water, being very soft, made the soap go a very long way.

It took me about five minutes to get wet, two

minutes to shower and about forty minutes to get rid of all the soap. Once finished, you had to take the head back off the hook and put it in the bath to avoid either freezing cold water or boiling hot, depending on which tap you switched off first. Washing my hair took for ever.

Drying took forever too; the dryer supplied couldn't have blown out the candles on a toddler's birthday cake. The switch had to be held down continuously, or it switched itself off, and with my hair, which is thick and long, taking a long time, it tired one thumb, then the other, then back again, and so on. By the time my hair was washed and dried, I needed to lie down in a darkened room and recover.

Footnote

The shower did have its day. When it was too rough to take a proper shower, I took a 'shath', or a 'bower'. Take your pick. Anyway, the shower did extremely well while I sat in the bath as the force was so little it was more controllable and I was scrunched up, so I was easier to soak. Much better than a shower; perhaps the cruise line was anticipating more rough days at sea than smooth days.

Just because most inanimate objects try to get at you when at your most vulnerable, naked, wet and in the bathroom, it doesn't end there. No, of course not. Leaving the bathroom, your cabin and even the ship will not insure you against the evil little bundles that are out to get you.

49

MORE INANIMATE OBJECTS

You know, naturally, that the backpack is distantly related to the cat. No? Oh yes, it is easily proved. Put twenty cat lovers in a room with one cat hater, introduce a cat, and the cat will straightaway make a beeline for the one hater. No amount of 'Here, kitty, kitty, come to (insert relevant name here), come and play,' from the lovers will make one jot of difference. Backpacks don't do quite the same, not being ambulant on their own, but it comes to the same. They were all provided at birth with backpack-hater-seeking magnets implanted under their fabric.

On cruises, you have to go to stately homes, castles,

cathedrals and museums in a group and most of these do not ban the backpack. They should, as they can wreak havoc when the owner isn't looking, which is most of the time, since they are, after all, BACKpacks and only teachers have eyes in the back of their heads, something we were all told as children.

So, the group trots round with a guide taking in all the wonderful sights, you look at the furniture, the walls and the floor, and lastly the ceiling. Suddenly people start taking steps backward, and then, just as you are thwacked round the face by a hostile backpack, you see them all lined up in the front row, knocking out all those without backpacks who are all standing in the back row. They always worm their way onto the back of a backpack lover and in front of a backpack hater and hit out. Just look next time you are in a crowd; all the backpacks will be at the front and all the handbag toters will be at the back with damaged faces.

It's quite fun to backpack watch in the trinket shop. Trinkets can fly everywhere, leaving the place looking like a battleground, and no one knows why or how or who, except you.

50

NOT FLEET ENOUGH

Disembarking is not always as easy as you would think. When you arrive for your cruise, you are given a swipe card with your name, your cabin number, the name of the ship and the title and duration of the cruise. You are then photographed. The photo does not appear on the card, but as you embark or disembark, the card is swiped and your photo comes up on a screen in front of the swiper (usually someone with little English as they do not usually speak much to the passengers) and you are clear to come or go. It's a good system, installed after a Greek ferry disaster when they were not sure of numbers. Occasionally it goes wrong and you hear a call for a passenger to identify themselves just before the ship leaves, but mostly it is pretty good.

We had never had a problem and had been several days on this cruise, so had no reason to think there was a problem now. We were off on an excursion and I handed over my swipe card.

'Isss not your card,' said the swiper. Oh dear, how had I managed it? I must have picked up Peter's by mistake. He handed back the card, and there was my name; it was my card.

'It is my card,' I told him.

'No isss not,' he insisted.

'But it is, look, that's my name there,' and I showed him.

'Isss not your photo.' Ah, that was different, I couldn't see the photo. If that was wrong, it was down to the computer.

'Can I see the photo please?' I asked. He swivelled the monitor, and a picture of Peter was smiling at me. Peter was behind me in the queue.

'That's me,' he said. 'Take my card, you may have a photo of my wife on it.' He took the card, swiped it and hey presto, a photo of me. 'The photos are just mixed up,' he continued. 'We'll get them sorted when we get back.'

'No, you go to reception now,' the swiper demanded.

'We can't go now, a coach is waiting for us,' explained Peter, reasonably.

'What's going on?' A chap in a senior officer's uniform had come over to see why the queue had come to a grinding halt. There was a short conversation in a foreign language; the senior seemed very relaxed, the junior very jobsworth. Peter's card was returned.

'Off you go,' said the senior, 'sort it out later.'

We went, had a good trip, arrived back and went to reception to sort out the cards. We explained what had happened and what the problem was.

'That's easy,' said the receptionist. He took the cards, did something on the computer and returned them.

Next day we were off again and the same jobsworth was at the swipe machine.

'Isss not your card,' he snarled.

'Yes it is,' I retorted, 'we sorted it out yesterday.'

'Not your card,' and he turned the monitor to me. This time all my details were wrong. My card had all of Peter's information on it, not just the photo. Instead of swapping the photos, the receptionist had swapped the information. The same senior was out in a flash.

'I know about this,' he chipped in. 'Let's have a look at your husband's card.' Peter submitted the card. It held all my information.

'Off you go,' he said to us. 'Reception will have to sort it out again, let's hope they get it right next time. Have a good trip.'

We fled. Back at reception we were issued with completely new cards. I went down to the gangway and offered my card to swipe, although I wasn't going anywhere. A different swiper swiped it and handed it back.

'Can I see the information please?' I asked. He looked puzzled; he didn't seem to understand. I tried another tack.

'What is the name on the card?' I asked.

'R... R... Mary Scott.' 'Rosalind' was clearly beyond him. Still, I had my answer; the swipe cards were now fine.

We had no bother after that.

It could also be difficult disembarking when a tour was called. The idea was, we went to the lounge, queued for a sticker to tell us which coach we were on, then waited in the lounge until that coach was called. Except that some people didn't. They crept down the stairs to the disembarkation point by the gangway and hovered there until there was a lull. They then had their cards swiped and rushed to the coach to sit on the front seat, long before the other passengers turned up from the lounge. Others registered that they were disabled in some way and had seats reserved for them, also at the front of the coach. We usually saw the same faces in the front seats. Not that we minded, with my being travel sick, I just wanted to sit towards the middle, between the wheels.

If we could, we sat opposite the middle entrance to the coach where there was usually a picture window. This worked well when it was just Peter and me, but with Mum, who walked slowly, we were often almost the last on the coach, and with three of us, we often had to sit at the back, separately.

On one cruise with Mum, we had several panoramic tours together, and each time we had to sit at the back. I began to feel sick and it was worse each day. Eventually, I decided to do something about it. I went to reception and explained what was happening and how I felt. The receptionist was most sympathetic.

'Were you on coach one today?' she asked.

'Yes,' I replied.

'I heard about that, did you wait to be called in the lounge?'

'Yes, we did.'

'Mm, I gather there were only about six of you left, all the others had already gone, what is it with the first coach?'

'Their elbows are sharper and their feet can kick further,' I suggested. 'To be honest, my husband and I prefer the last coach. It usually isn't full, and the people are more relaxed, but my mother-in-law always goes for the first one.'

'Tell you what I'll do, tomorrow it's a tender port, which excursion are you on?' I told her. 'There are two coaches for that tour, they'll both be on the first tender, Joe is the Trekkers escort on one. I'll tell him your situation, then find him in the lounge and go with him to the tender, and he'll tell you what to do.'

I thanked her and left. The following morning we

waited in the lounge and I saw a Trekkers escort (they wore a uniform of sorts) by the door, I went up to him and told him who I was and what had happened. He told me to stay by the door and that I was to leave with him at the front of the queue. I let Peter and Mum know what was happening.

When the tender was called, I walked with the escort, Joe, through the door. As I approached the stairs, an elderly gentleman with a walking stick tucked under his arm dodged in front of me, but behind Joe, and with his walking stick stuck out at an angle, so I couldn't get by. On the next landing was another man on the other side of the stairs doing the same thing. My way was blocked and already I had lost sight of Joe. Several other people with various armaments blocking the way appeared on the stairs. I was completely stymied.

I reached the bottom of the stairs, and Joe was waiting. He didn't look happy.

'Let the lady through,' he ordered. No one moved. I was still stuck.

'Let the lady through,' he repeated. Still no one moved. He stood there silently.

'No one is going until you let the lady through,' he commanded. Grumbles ensued. Who did I think I was? Mumble, mumble, but they let me through. Eleven people had pushed in front on the stairs. I went up to Joe. He went through the card swiper and I followed. So did two others and by the time I had got to the gangway, they were both ahead, having elbowed me out of the way with sticks and backpacks. The tender waited at the bottom of the gangway. Joe was already on it, standing, blocking the doorway.

'Let the lady on first,' he said in a masterly teacher's voice. They gave in, reluctantly.

'Sit by the door,' he told me, 'Keep a space by you for your husband. Your mother-in-law can sit the other side of the door with me.' I nodded agreement and placed my front-back pack on the seat beside me.

People poured in. My feet were trodden on, I was dug with bags and baggage, my hat was knocked over my face, and I felt thoroughly battered. I had to keep telling passengers my husband was going to sit next to me to keep the space free for him. Joe had to keep pushing people off the seat by the door on the other side; it was incredible.

At last (well, almost last) Peter and Mum arrived and managed to sit where Joe wanted them. Everyone else sat down. The tender was cast off and Joe sat down too.

Arriving at the jetty, nearly everyone stood up. 'Sit down,' yelled Joe, and some passengers sat. 'Sit down!' he repeated. Everyone sat.

'Let the lady off first.'

'Why her?' I heard. I stood warily, wondering who was going to take me out at the knees.

'Okay,' said Joe, 'off you go Rose, to coach number one.' I got off and ran. I arrived at the coach, and guess what, there were people there before me. I had arrived on the first tender, how had they done that? I later found out they had arrived and gone across with the staff on the grounds that they had permission because they were disabled. Luckily for me, they all wanted to sit at the front, so I had the choice of anywhere between the front and back wheels and was able to sit in the middle.

Peter and I now have a good method. We wait until the coach before ours is called, then make our way to the back of the lounge. Peter waits at the back, I walk on to the top of the stairs where I can still see Peter; he waits until we are called, waves to me and I run down the stairs to arrive at the coach early. I am never first, but I am usually the first to want to sit in the middle. It has worked so far.

51

WATER, WATER EVERYWHERE

I know all there is to know about the Pacific Ocean. This is because I have travelled across it in both directions and in the north and the south. From leaving a port on one side of the ocean to arriving at a port on the other, I have yet to see another vessel. I have only seen them in or near port. I therefore conclude that nothing useful actually crosses the Pacific Ocean. As our largest and deepest ocean, it is not fit for purpose. All it does is keep Asia away from North America and Australasia from South America. We could do that for ourselves, if we were only big enough. Should there be targets to be met concerning the Pacific, they would be missed. It must follow that it should be filled in and used for growing crops or building houses. We saw plenty of aeroplanes crossing the Pacific. If it was filled in, the people who now fly could walk.

However, although there are thousands of square miles of ocean which are completely empty, whenever Peter and I stepped into a tender, which as we all know, in another life is a lifeboat, we nearly always hit another vessel; another lifeboat. Lifeboats either come with huge magnets hidden somewhere, or they are of two sexes, constantly seeking out each other for a quick cuddle. We would arrive at a port after days at sea, embark a tender and before we knew it, it would either hit another tender, or the jetty, or the ship we were leaving. Tenders must have the worst record for accidents in the ocean, which is a bit sobering since you are supposed to trust your life to them when there is nothing else available.

On one famous occasion we were to be off the ship by tender at 7.30 am. Breakfast only started at 0700, but with a scramble, we were in the lounge by 7.30. We waited and waited... then waited some more. Dolphins, lots of pods, were sighted just about everywhere around the ship. Hundreds of them, it seemed, but still we waited. Eventually, all the other groups with later start times had caught up with us in the lounge. It grew very full, and the inmates became restless. At 0800, the 22 of us on the first excursion were called to the tender. We arrived downstairs – no tender, just the captain, looking fraught.

We were sent to the other side of the ship, where there was a tender. It was bouncing up and down like nothing on earth, and it took a minute or so to board each passenger. Once on, we waited again and eventually left. At this point, the engine stopped, and one wag said, 'What a time to run out of petrol'.

At last, the engine fired. It became clear immediately that the pilot had not the first idea where we were going despite the fact that the channel markers were clearly visible from the ship, as was the landing stage. We now realised why the dolphins had stayed round; just for a laugh. We went left (or rather, port); we went right (or rather, starboard); we went round in circles and we were no nearer land. The pilot got annoyed (the passengers were not too pleased either). Lots of gesticulating, and shouting in Tagalag (one of the languages of the Philippines). The crew became angrier, trying to tell the pilot what to do, more shouting. Another tender came alongside to tell him where to go (the passengers were up for telling him where to go too). He didn't go where the other tender said, though, he merely hit it. This must have been extremely difficult to do in an empty ocean, yet he managed to hit the only obstacle around.

More shouting and gesticulating, this time from the two crews, more going left and right, while the other tender beat a hasty retreat. We did a few more circles.

People were beginning to look and feel seasick; others looked ready to jump overboard. Steam was emerging from some ears. It was amazing just how many passengers had been in the Navy and knew exactly what to do. Several nautical engineers knew also, and others, including canoeists, kayakers and dinghyists, put in their two pennorth; lively conversations were struck up all around the tender. The pilot ignored it all. At one point we thought we were going back to the ship.

Eventually, between three of the crew, we managed to hit the landing stage several times before we tied up. It had taken three quarters of an hour for a ten-minute ride, and we still had to be released from the ordeal.

52

THERE'S MANY A SLIP

Cruise lines can be surprising. Their itineraries are set at least two years ahead, and although weather can alter plans at the last minute, mostly the cruise is plain sailing, as it were. Just occasionally though, they seem to be caught out by the most obvious of features. Tender ports are always tricky as the ship has to anchor out at sea and the reason for there not being a proper port may well be tides, currents, winds or the poverty of the island. So, we always expect the unexpected if tendering. Otherwise we don't worry — the cruise line has had it all planned for years.

We once boarded a cruise which included a visit to Mont St Michel. It was the featured picture on the cruise line's brochure, it was featured on the page of the outline and it was featured on the front of the excursion booklet. It was the highlight of the cruise; the port lecturer said so, so it had to be true. We were eagerly anticipating landing in St Malo the following day for our excursion to the island. Then there was an announcement that the tide was all wrong for us to land in St Malo and we would be omitting that stop.

Now I'm not trying to teach grandma to suck eggs, but hadn't the relevant people checked the tides beforehand? I know tides are like Easter and move about a bit, but just like Easter, they are completely predictable, so what was the problem really, that we were only told less than 24 hours beforehand? To this day I have no idea.

The Severn Bore is a well-known feature; it arrives on cue, a spectacular event with swimmers and surfboarders taking advantage. We know it will happen, so how come people who should know about this type of thing don't?

We were on a ship moored on the River Seine, well north of Paris. We had an excursion in the morning and arrived back at the ship for lunch. Trouble was, we were not allowed back. The ship was shut. We were told we could not come back on board until after a bore had passed, as it might be dangerous to be on board when it struck. No one had mentioned this at breakfast; it appeared to have manifested itself out of nothing.

We waited at the gangway, looking down the river to see this phenomenon. No one near us had seen a bore before and we were all excited; this was going to be worth missing lunch for. We waited and watched. The time of the bore came and went (yes, suddenly they knew all about it). Was it late? We watched and waited some more and then were let onto the ship. We hadn't seen it yet, we protested, we wanted to stay outside and photograph it. It was all over, we were told, it was only five centimetres in height, just a ripple, and hadn't we noticed it? The bore no one knew about at breakfast had become dangerous to shipping by lunchtime and then died just as we were warming up. For that, they closed the ship. Lunch was a murderous affair.

Weeks are similar. We know there are usually about seven days in a week and roughly fifty-two weeks in a year, and the itinerary is set by date and day well in advance so we know if we are landing at a port on a Sunday. We went on a trip one Sunday, and hey presto, all the places we were supposed to visit were closed; it was a Roman Catholic country, so I had a pretty good idea before we went that shops would be shut, but so was a garden, a museum, the lavatories and a wine tasting. That didn't leave a lot. In fact, it left nothing, as we couldn't visit the church either.

Mostly though, it goes well, and the excursions are

accompanied by a local guide and a cruise line escort, who, between them keep us in order and entertain us. I say mostly; the best local guide we have ever had was in the Orkneys, and when we asked her how long she had been a guide she told us we were her first ever group. I hope she is still doing the same job and enthusing her audience as she enthused us.

The worst local guide we ever had was on the Isle of Man. Our trip was a panoramic tour of the island with a stop for shopping at a craft centre, another stop for the parliament and a final stop at a picturesque seaside town. We were with Mum. Our cruise escort was a lively young gentleman from the entertainments department, but the local tour guide was a somewhat aged gentleman resembling a poorly-fed turtle. Maybe he was filling in for someone else at the last minute, but it didn't go well.

We left the port, passing an enormous Tesco store. Talking at about one syllable a second in a complete monotone, he said, 'That's Tesco there, you can see it, the big white building on the left.' We could see it all right; we could see it from the ship. A big clue was that it said TESCO on the side, and I think I am right in assuming we could all read.

With Tesco well behind us now, he continued, 'Half the population of the island live in the main town, so the same number of people live in the town as in all the rest of the island put together.' there was a long pause while we were given time to digest this fact, and he continued, 'Half the population are men, so the other half are women.' He waited again, in case we had difficulty understanding this gem. We did wonder about children, but didn't ask. He told us there were 365 churches on the island, so if we wanted to we could visit a different church every day for a year, unless it was a leap year, and if it was, we would have to go without for one day; there was another pause. In fact he said nothing else until we arrived at the craft centre.

'Here is the stop for the craft centre, but it has been closed for several months, you have half an hour here,' he said.

We alighted from the bus to see a ramshackle crop of terrapin huts, all shut up and empty, all in need of a great deal of work, paint peeling, windows hanging at odd angles, doors padlocked, set in an overgrown car park sporting a huge collection of rosebay willow herb and buddleia. We looked around for something to do for half an hour. There wasn't anything. We spoke to the cruise escort, who decided we should continue to another stop. The local guide didn't like that; we were scheduled to stop there for half an hour and that is what we should do. The driver joined in on the side of the escort and most of the passengers. Mum was very peeved; she was going to buy some Christmas presents, where could she buy them now? We all joined in; we wanted to continue. The local guide was adamant; we were staying. The driver decided he was driving off. If the guide wanted to stay he could, but the rest of us were leaving. We left, and unfortunately the guide came with us.

The next stop was the parliament site. The passengers at the front wanted to ask questions, but the guide was having none of it. We proceeded in silence, eventually arriving at the site, where there was a small museum.

'The museum is over there,' the guide explained, waving his arm roughly in the direction of a small brick-built building. 'All your questions will be answered inside, you can read about it.' And that was it. That was our introduction, lecture and summary of the one of the oldest parliaments in the world. He gave a key to the escort to open the museum and remained on the bus. We trooped over to the museum and trooped out again, working out the history between us. His only contribution as we left the coach was, 'It's all in the museum.'

The driver did what he could, which was quite a lot, and he helped us understand how traditions were built up and how the parliament worked today. Mum even complained, and she was usually quite happy to be left alone on the bus without a running commentary. She had had a good nap on the bus, and was beginning to feel lively.

Back on the bus, and we were off to the seaside. Mum was looking forward to this; a cup of coffee in a coffee shop and a browse round the rest of the shops.

Maybe she would be able to buy those Christmas presents after all.

The cruise escort asked if anyone had any questions for the local guide. He was asked about property prices and told us they were three or four times the price of those in the UK. The driver corrected him and said they were about the same price. Oh dear! I asked about the island's relationship with the EU, since it wasn't a member, but it was geographically very close and I had heard it had close links with Norway.

'Ah,' he said slowly, even for him, 'The relationship is this. My wife was born on the island and can't work in the EU. I was born in the UK, so I can.' and that was the sum total of his explanation.

Suddenly (that's the wrong word, nothing was sudden with him), he became more animated. 'We are travelling down the most important street on the island,' he said. Immediately those who were nearly asleep (most people) perked up, except Mum, who was dead to the world. The rest of us were all ears. This was almost exciting.

'Yes, my mother-in-law lives here, in that house there,' he said, and he pointed it out. 'I call my mother-in-law MIL,' he explained, 'you see, mother-in-law, the initials are M, I and L, so I call her MIL. I am her son-in-law, so guess what she calls me? She calls me SIL, that's short for son-in-law, S, I and L are the initials of son-in-law. That means we are MIL and SIL, see?'

Did I say almost exciting? We were giving up the will to live again. We proceeded more or less in silence to the last stop.

'I want a coffee,' announced Mum. To be honest, I was surprised she didn't ask for something stronger. I'm almost teetotal and he could have driven me to drink. We sat and drank in the shade (Mum didn't like sunshine) and debated whether we had the energy to explore the shops. We explored one or two and wandered back to the coach, where the driver was chatting to several passengers.

We usually give the local guide a tip – they usually more than earn it. That day we gave it straight to the driver.

53

FOOD FOR THOUGHT

A Rhine cruise through Europe. We liked the look of it, a small boat, luxurious dining and time to see the castles and picture postcard towns we had heard about. We booked twice, one year for a normal cabin and a second in one of the two magnificent cabins at the back (neither was available for the first year).

We arrived, unpacked and decided to have a drink before dinner. No one was manning the bar, so we waited, along with other people with the same idea.

A waiter arrived. 'I don't normally do the bar, but the bar staff have all left,' he said, and proceeded to serve. We thought it odd that some staff had left during a cruise, and thought it must have been because their contracts were tied in to a date, rather than the cruises. He was an efficient barman and we thought no more about it.

It has to be said that we were disappointed in our first meal afloat. The carafes of water on the tables were no doubt clean, but they were covered in white speckles left after constant use in hard water. The meal itself was very cabbagey - cabbage soup, two types of cabbage as vegetables with the main course. Not very imaginative, and slowly and not attractively served.

The next morning, breakfast looked better; there was more choice, no cabbages. Peter likes toast at breakfast, while I like croissants and Danish pastries. He went off to make his toast. A loaf was provided which you cut yourself and fed your slices into a toaster.

I hadn't yet picked up my croissant when Peter appeared at my side. 'Come and look at this,' he whispered urgently. I followed him to the bread. He showed me what he had cut and what was left. It was covered in mould. We cut the loaf further along; it was completely mouldy. We called the head waitress and showed her. 'Oh my God!' was the response, and she lifted the loaf out and disappeared with it.

I suggested Peter had a croissant. He declined, but I went back to them. They were displayed in a basket with a napkin lining it. I lifted the napkin; the basket was mouldy. This time, I called the maître d'. I showed him the basket. 'It's only in the corners,' he said and walked off.

I found the cruise director, Dawn, and told her about both incidents. She had arrived on board with us the day before and was as horrified as we were.

She disappeared into the kitchen and arrived back in few minutes. 'I didn't see the bread, but I threw the basket out,' she said.

As the week progressed, we had more varieties of cabbage, served slowly and sullenly. One evening, the cabbage soup had half an apple in the bottom. We weren't sure what we were supposed to do with it, since only spoons were provided for soup. We finished up leaving the apples, but wondered if they would come back as apple soup, perhaps with a cabbage in the bottom. During the week, members of the crew disappeared off the boat whenever we stopped, so service became even slower. In the end, half way through our two-week cruise, the captain left.

That night, I chose pasta for my main course as I was growing tired of cabbage, and they couldn't put cabbage with pasta, could they? The menu said pasta with bacon and cheese and a lemon sauce. The pasta arrived, a mountain of it. I counted five pieces of bacon, each a centimetre square. Of the cheese, there was no sign, but there was a puddle of something yellow. I took a mouthful. Yuck! It tasted like the bergamot suntan lotion I used to cover myself in before it was withdrawn for possibly being carcinogenic. Not that I drank the stuff, but when I wiped it on my face, I would cover my lips and that was when I could taste it. I called the maitre d'.

'I can't eat this, it tastes like suntan lotion,' I complained. He shrugged his shoulders unhelpfully, so I called Dawn. She looked at my mountain and asked me what it was supposed to be. She said a new captain would be arriving the next day and if we could all hang on, he would sort out the kitchen and the dining room where the service was so awful.

Without eating a main course, I chose tiramisu for pudding. When it came, it came with a sauce. Which sauce would you put with tiramisu, if you had to? Coffee? Chocolate? Cream? No. It was served with MINT sauce. Well, it was mint jelly, but it was the mint that did it. No one ate it.

The following day, Dawn sent for Peter and me. The new captain had arrived, and was hoping new staff would be arriving in a day or two to replace those haemorrhaging from the boat currently. He listened to our dissatisfaction with the dining room and kitchen, and to our unstinting praise for everyone else on the boat; the stewards, cleaners, deck crew and Dawn herself, who had tried to do so much to help, but was thwarted by a group of staff who would not change. The captain gave us a bottle of wine and suggested that as we had already booked for the same boat the next year, we should write to the cruise line too.

Things improved under the new captain, but of course, we were stuck with the food on board. In order to improve the service, we had to order our next meal at the previous meal and the starter would be on the table as we arrived. Not ideal, and we tended to forget what we had ordered and it might not get to quite the right spot on the table, leading to swaps. And cabbages still took centre stage. We actually went to look for a McDonald's when we stopped in one small German town. However, it was a lovely cruise, the company was great and the cabin comfortable and spotlessly clean. We came home ready to laugh about it. We did write to the cruise line however, and were promised a different staff and delicious food the next year.

One year later

Cruising from Amsterdam to the Black Sea includes some time on canals. We were on the same boat as the previous year, not tall, but even so, too tall to go under the bridges over the canal we were travelling on. One day, we were to go under almost thirty bridges and the roof was lowered for most of the day. When lowering the roof, the funnel had also to be lowered.

We were on a lovely boat; all the cabins were comfortable, but there were two at the back which were especially luxurious, with patio doors allowing us a view of where we had just been. The door led to a balcony with loungers and chairs. It was gorgeous, and so relaxing. We had one of these cabins, and the other couple at our dining table had the other. We had lots in common with them and enjoyed their company for meals.

On the day the roof and the funnels came down, we sat outside admiring the view, Peter went off to sleep and I read my book, occasionally waving to people on the towpath and taking photos I went in to make a cup of tea. As I went into the room, I noticed my clothes were covered in smuts. I went back out and Peter's clothes were smutty too. Looking up, we saw the funnel that had been lowered had been diverted to two small pipes, one ending just above our balcony, and the other above next door.

After tea, I changed and took my trousers down to the cruise director and explained what had happened.

'Don't worry,' he said (Dawn had left by now), 'send your trousers to the laundry, I'll get you a bag for them,' and he disappeared, arriving back with a large white plastic bag. I took the bag back to the cabin, so we could put both pairs of trousers in it, while I washed our tee shirts. I arrived back at the cabin, and read what was written on the bag. 'No responsibility can be taken for some stains which cannot be removed, shrinkage, damage, loss or colour fastness.' I read it out to Peter.

'I'm not sending my Versace trousers to be cleaned here, they don't take responsibility for anything,' I said to Peter and he agreed, but decided to send his. They came back the next day, beautifully clean and pressed. We also received a bottle of champagne 'for your inconvenience', but it was addressed to someone else!

I went next door to our friends, whom we knew only by their first names, and asked if it was them. It was. Management must have been confused, so we invited them in to share the champagne. They suggested they should sit out on our balcony, get themselves smutty and earn another bottle, but they didn't do it.

54

GULLS, WASPS AND OTHER IRRITATING CREATURES

Another restaurant, another beverage; tea this time, as it was late afternoon and Mum lived by coffee in the morning and tea in the afternoon. It was September, so the sun was low on the horizon.

We arrived in the car park and left the coach. The restaurant had seating inside and out, but we knew Mum would want to sit inside; she hated eating outdoors, picnics and eating al fresco were anathema to her. On this occasion we would have made the same choice ourselves, September being a wonderful month for wasps and midges.

We picked our way across the car park, which adjoined the outside eating area. This had been taken over by the young-mums-with-babies-in-a-buggy-brigade; the mums were talking into their mobiles, while the babies were systematically throwing everything they could find within reach out of the buggies. We avoided plastic models, bits of comfort blanket, bottles, teats, car keys... car keys? We also avoided the child who had managed to find a half-used loaf of sliced bread (presumably for ducks somewhere) and was throwing slices with gay abandon all around. No ducks had arrived yet, but gulls of all types and descriptions were fighting over the spoils.

The young mums, oblivious to all this, continued to talk into their mobiles. They had it all worked out; the tables were the picnic variety with the seats as inbuilt benches. A young mum sat at each table with various packages and appendages spread on the seat or table (or, of course, both) while the buggies were set in between the tables so no one could sit anywhere near. Fortunately, as we drew nearer, we could see lots of space inside the restaurant.

We waited in the queue; Peter took up the rear with a tray, Mum was in the middle and I was at the front with the MasterCard. Mum began to lean on me, which I bore until we were next in line to serve, then I suggested she find a table while Peter and I did the rest. She toddled off. Once served, I couldn't see Mum anywhere, and neither could Peter. Then we spied her outside. We couldn't understand it. There was lots of room inside; why had she gone out? We caught up with her, and watched the young mums, who were in various stages of removal.

'Why are you out here?' asked Peter.

'I want to sit outside.' Mum was quite emphatic.

Eventually, one young mum outdid the rest and retrieved all her belongings (and hopefully the car keys) and moved. This made space on one side of a table as long as Mum could shimmy past a buggy, avoid being thrown at by the baby inside and manage to negotiate the bench seat. We assumed she would sit there, but she didn't.

'I can't sit there,' she said.

'Well, wait a moment,' I put in, 'the buggy will go in a minute.'

'I can't sit there,' Mum insisted. 'The sun's in my eyes.'

'I think we ought to go inside,' I said, ducking to avoid being dive-bombed by a gull.

'If we sit that side, Mum can sit on the other, then her back would be to the sun,' Peter suggested.

'We'll have to wait for that buggy to go,' I added, looking at a particularly ferocious child who did not like his face being wiped by his mother and was letting her know it.

So we all changed sides and sat down. A wasp arrived, then two, then three. Mum started flapping violently with her napkin. The wasps became agitated;

Mum became even more agitated. We had told Mum to leave wasps alone so many times, but it made no difference. The tea cups were perilously near the firing line.

'We ought to go inside,' said Peter, very definitely. So that's what we did.

55

ARISTOCRATIC ANASTASIA

I felt sorry for Anastasia; she wanted to make friends and hadn't a clue how. When she opened her mouth, what came out just upset those around.

It was the first night on one of our earliest cruises. We all arrived at the table at about the same time and sat down - Anastasia was on my left, Peter on my right – and we kept those positions all cruise. There were seven of us and we hadn't even said hello. I later learned the others at the table were a married couple, John and Joan, and two sisters, Kath and Pat. Anastasia was a slim thirty-something with messy, mousey hair and a gap between her front teeth, like Jilly Cooper. The evening started with her question.

'I say, does anybody here hunt?' she said in a cut-glass accent. There was no reply, although I am pretty sure we all heard. The hunting ban hadn't come into force then, but hunting was a hot potato at Westminster at the time, and on cruises, you just didn't talk about hot potatoes. This one was only a short cruise, a fly cruise for a week in the Mediterranean, and it was unlikely that by the end of the week we would know our table companions' politics or their religion. We would know little else about them other than places they had visited, a little about their immediate family and their hobbies. All safe stuff.

'Oh, none of you,' she continued, looking round at us. 'I keep foxhounds, four of them, and I find hunting thrilling, I'm passionate about it.'

Nowadays, everyone is 'passionate' about the most trivial of things, like socks or cup hooks or bamboo sticks. Twenty years ago, it was a word used mainly for steamy sex and little else. Anastasia felt 'passionate' about hunting? Well I never!

Still no one said anything, so she ploughed on. 'I go with my sponsor, my sponsor suggested I came on this cruise, I'm here to get a man.'

'Your sponsor? What's that?' asked a lady whose name we later found out was Kath.

It turned out that Anastasia was having an affair with a married man, and he had suggested the cruise. It was never quite clear as to whether he had also thought she should look for a man. We did get the impression that maybe he was trying to release himself from her. She wasn't one to spot subtlety; if he wanted to get rid of her, I think he would have to unceremoniously dump her. She might not even notice then.

Kath steered the conversation into more general topics and hunting took a back seat, if you can do that with hunting. The next night Anastasia continued in the same vein.

'Don't you think that horses are just the most frightfully good animals?' Yes, she really did say 'frightfully', and she should have left it there, but she continued, 'They're so much nicer than those donkey creatures.'

Now I like just about anything that has legs, particularly if you can't train it, and I love donkeys. They are clever, they have a sense of humour and you can't fool them. They also work hard, but they won't do a thing unless they want to. You can meet your match with a donkey. I wasn't going to let Anastasia's statement go.

As I raised my head to speak, I noticed Joan had blushed to the roots of her hair; not knowing her, I had no idea why, but I spoke out anyway,

'I love donkeys,' I said. 'They have much more sensible ears than horses [why did I say that?] and they're intelligent. Put a jump in the middle of a donkey paddock and the donkey will look at it, see there is nothing all round and walk round it. You'd never get a donkey jumping over something it didn't need to.'

Silence. No one quite knew what to say next, but I did notice Joan nodding. Anastasia hadn't finished.

'There's this fabulous man on the cruise, I got talking to him today, he's going to watch the show and I'm going to sit with him. Kath, Pat, will you join me?'

'I don't watch the shows.' This from Pat. 'I like to read in my cabin.'

'Kath, will you come? I'd like some moral support,'

'I don't really want to be a gooseberry,' said Kath.

'Oh, you won't be, don't worry.' Anastasia started giving Kath instructions on where and when they should meet. Kath looked very doubtful about it but at last, after some wheedling, she did agree.

After the meal, John and Joan sought us out. 'That girl makes me mad,' said Joan, beginning to blush again. 'I sponsor and help out at a donkey sanctuary at the weekends. What she said about donkeys... she's awful.'

Now I knew what the blushing was all about. The four of us chatted, then went our separate ways. Peter and I went down to the show and watched it from near the back. After about twenty minutes, we saw Anastasia coming towards us,

'God, he's an awful bore,' she said loudly. She presumably meant the 'fabulous man' she had met.

'Have you left Kath with him?' I asked.

'Yes, she'll be fine, I'm off,' and with that, she left.

After the show, Kath came by. She was fuming. 'That's the last time I do anything for her,' she ranted. 'She left me with him after a couple of minutes. I didn't feel I could go too. She's so insensitive.'

'Anastasia is doing well,' I commented, 'first Joan and now Kath.'

'It's going to be a cheery table,' remarked Peter.

The next day, dinner was the usual, with Anastasia kicking off. 'I was on a tour today with some of those awful people who work in factories,' she declared to the table at large. I noticed Joan, who was blushing again. I changed the subject, asking which tours people were going the following day; John and Joan would be with us. We agreed it would be pleasant and we would try to sit near each other on the coach.

After dinner, they crept up behind us, Joan saying, 'I am so mad, I work in a factory, and I do highly skilled work. I work in a carpet factory, and occasionally, the looms get muddled and the pattern goes wrong. I have to unhook the carpet, take it back by hand, re-establish the pattern by hand and set it back on the loom. It is really difficult, takes years to master, and I am proud to do what I do. How dare she belittle me?' She was furious, and so was John, and hearing that, so were we.

Joan was almost in tears. 'She's having an affair with a married man, how can she be so judgemental, the hussy?'

John laughed and dug her in the ribs. 'You can't get

through to people like that, ignore her, I do,' he said, and they went on their way.

It was nearing the end of the cruise when Anastasia first seemed to realise she was not popular. After nattering on about 'the estate' and 'the staff' – reserving all her respect for the former – she moaned, 'No one here likes me, Kath is angry with me, which makes Pat angry with me. Joan doesn't like me which means John doesn't like me. I can't do anything right.'

'Have you thought of jumping overboard?' I asked.

The bruise on my right ankle took weeks to clear up.

56

A CAUTIONARY TALE

A friend told me this story. It may be true, it may be an urban legend, but it illustrates the lengths people will go to to sit at the front of a coach.

A group of people were going on a coach tour of Europe. You know the kind of thing; if it's Friday it must be Italy. Anyway, they met up at a hotel for the first night and the next morning, after breakfast, they were catching the coach for two weeks of sightseeing. The coach duly drew up, and the passengers gathered in the car park. The tour escort introduced herself and said before they alighted that they would all take it in turns to sit at the front, as she knew this was always a popular seat and it was only fair to let everyone have the chance to take good photos from the front of the coach.

Two ladies who were travelling together waved at her, gaining her attention.

'Yes,' she said, 'what can I do?'

'Well,' one of them said, 'we have to sit in the front seats because we are both travel sick.'

'Oh, dear,' she replied, 'I am so sorry, you must have been given the wrong information, but it doesn't matter, I can do something about it right now. It is such a pity you have wasted a night in the hotel for nothing. You see this is a coach holiday, and you will be on a coach every day for twelve days in succession. Clearly, if you are both travel sick, you cannot possibly come with us, but I can send for a taxi right now to take you to the station before the rest of us leave. If you can show how you came to have the wrong information when you booked the holiday and you check it all with the small print, you may even be able to have your money back, but I'm not certain about that. I suggest you go back into the hotel now with your luggage and I'll be with you in a moment.'

'Oh, no it's all right, we'll still come,' the ladies agreed. They left their luggage to be loaded, climbed on the bus with everyone else, and didn't make a fuss about sharing the front seat with everyone else in their turn. Neither of them was travel sick, no matter where they sat.

57

DON'T FORGET THE WATER

The sun had been blazing in a clear blue sky for days. The ship was in Libya, cruising along the North African coast. The days were hot and the Roman remains promised to be spectacular. The port lecturer was talking to us about Cyrene, one of the excursions for the following day.

'Whatever you do, remember to take bottled water with you,' he said. 'Firstly, you must keep up your liquid intake, as the Sahara can be incredibly hot, and secondly, the Sahara sand covers everything, including the fine mosaics you will see. If you sprinkle water onto the mosaics, you will see the colour come up. They are beautiful.'

We were not going to Cyrene, we were off to Leptis Magna, just along the coast, but we wished we had more time so that we could see Cyrene too. However, our friends were going there and we could compare notes later, at dinner.

We set off the next morning in a ramshackle old bus with windows held on by string and all the stuffing falling out of the seats. Black smoke followed us as the engine coughed and whined and seemed on the verge of giving up. Libya hadn't really got into the tourist thing yet, but give it time, its two neighbours had got it off to a fine art.

We arrived; Leptis Magna was unbelievable, a huge complex of glorious Roman grandeur. Could anything be better than this? We walked miles to cover the ancient city and the amphitheatre, and heard stories of the Romans and the conservation of the UNESCO heritage site. We ate our packed lunch in the open, under the sun and soaked in all the culture we could. The afternoon was just as spectacular. We had to take the coach to another part of the site, it was so large, and we were overwhelmed by the skill of the craftsmen and the foresight of the planners. A never-to-be-forgotten day, but sadly, not a venue the British can go to any more. Let's hope it isn't all destroyed during the current turmoil.

We dressed for dinner full of our day, bursting to tell our friends who were going there for a short tour the next day all about it, and agog to hear about Cyrene. We arrived at the table first. They arrived, and to say they did not look excited was an understatement. They looked world weary as they dropped into their chairs.

'Oh, it's good to be back,' commented Charles.

'What a day,' said Tina, 'it's nice to be warm at last.'

We asked what had happened and heard this story. They had set off, just after we had, in the morning for their full day tour. The bus, if anything, was even worse than ours. Some of the windows were completely absent, while others looked as though they would fall out if breathed on, and the engine was clearly in a terrible state.

The bus rattled off, not along the coast like ours, but towards the south, to the interior towards the Sahara Desert. It had been beautiful weather, and knowing they were going towards the Sahara, most of the party thought it would be very hot. Hadn't the lecturer warned us it might be hot, only yesterday?

As they went south, they ascended into the mountains, where it became colder and colder. The sky grew overcast and by the time they arrived at Cyrene it looked thunderous. They alighted and the skies opened. They found out later that four inches of rain had fallen on them in twenty minutes. Most of them were wearing sandals, shorts and tee shirts, with sun hats; very few had macs or umbrellas, and they were completely drenched. The rain continued, on and off, all day. The temperature was in single digits Celsius and they were fed up. Lunch was taken in a cavern on the site. This was cold, damp and eerie and still the rain drenched it all.

They dripped and splashed their way around in the afternoon, shivering, teeth chattering and feeling thoroughly miserable. At last, it was time to come home. Perhaps they'd dry off in the coach. They climbed aboard, noticing that the seats were wet. As they bounced along the road home, the rain increased and started to drive in through the windows in the ceiling of the coach, as none of them closed properly. The temperature didn't rise again until they were almost back on the coast.

They arrived back chilled to the bone, and it wasn't until they had taken showers that they began to feel better. They both chose soup for the first course and began to smile about it. We kept quiet about Leptis Magna.

The next day, the port lecturer apologised. Since that day, no matter what the weather, no matter how silly we look, as well as bottles of water, we always take our cagoules everywhere. If we don't need to use them, they are useful to keep on our seats in the coach, just in case anyone is tempted to steal them.

58

ANOTHER CAUTIONARY TALE

At the end of a cruise, I sometimes have clothing I don't want to take back home. Our litter bin on the last night occasionally looks like the remnants of a jumble sale. On any cruise, you have to pack the day before you arrive back in dock. You put out your suitcases before midnight, and during the night they are collected for offloading into the terminal building before you have breakfast. You keep a small case with you for your nightwear and toiletries. As you leave the ship, you pick up your cases in the terminal building and off you go. Easy. Of course, things can go wrong...

Mum did her packing in her cabin, we did ours in ours. Peter reminded me that I should have all my clothes for the next day. I checked and having been a girl guide, I laid them all out in the order I would be wearing them, from bra and briefs to shoes and jacket, and checked they were all present and correct. Peter did the same.

We finished our packing and went to dinner, casual tonight as all the posh clothes were probably already in their cases. We said our goodbyes and hoped we would meet our friends the next morning before we departed. After the evening entertainment we went to bed, having secured the cases and put in as much as we possibly could. It was at this point I decided that my sandals were a bit the worse for wear and I would leave them behind. We put the cases out in the corridor and went to bed.

Next morning, we saw our stewardess and told her we were off to breakfast and we wouldn't mind her starting on the room straightaway. We knew how hectic the changeover day was, and although we had to be out of the cabin by 8 am, we were always happy for her to start cleaning and changing the bedding before that. We popped down the corridor to Mum. We knocked on her door, and she opened it.

'I've packed my shoes,' she wailed. We looked at her feet. She was wearing the towelling flip flops the cruise company provided in the cabin. She never normally wore them as she had had operations on her toes and could not keep mule-type shoes on her feet as she couldn't curl her toes.

'Not to worry,' I said, 'I've left my sandals, you can have them to wear' (we both took a 6). I went back to our cabin. No stewardess and no rubbish; she had gone off with it. I trotted off down the corridor, calling for her; no reply. I went along, passing all the cabins she serviced; no luck. I went back.

'I can't find the stewardess anywhere, she's gone off with the rubbish,' I called. Peter and I left Mum and went off in different directions. I eventually saw the stewardess along the corridor. 'Have you still got our rubbish? Mum packed her shoes and hasn't got anything to wear on her feet.' I wasn't very hopeful, as the bin bag on her trolley looked empty.

She immediately ran off. I waited; she was gone a good ten minutes. I was just imagining Mum flipping and flopping her way home in the cruise line slippers; at least we would be in a car door to door. I had nearly given up hope, but eventually the stewardess reappeared, with the sandals and a grin on her face. Thank goodness I was offloading sandals. If they had been trainers Mum would probably have refused to wear them.

Mum never packed her shoes in error again.

59

THE KNOWLEDGE OF THE ANCIENT MARINER

The general knowledge quizzes each day on cruises always create much interest. There are usually about 20 questions and the average winning number is somewhere around 14, sometimes as low as 8, which gives you some idea of the obscurity of the questions. We mark our own papers and if you're lucky (or unlucky, you might say) the prize is a key ring or an unrefillable pen with the cruise company logo on it. For such amazing generosity the competition is fierce. Peter and I have been known to win, but not often.

The quizmaster always had tales of cheats, including the two ex-teachers who always scored 20, even on a day when they were late and missed the first three clues, which were not repeated. He couldn't understand why they had cheated for such paltry prizes, but competitive people will always be competitive, no matter what, and ex-teachers? Well, they probably want everyone to think they know everything.

We were on the *Beeline Bounty* when we met Gavin. He had a mobile home near Southampton, but lived on the *Bounty* from October to May every year. Beeline had been made a special name badge for him, calling him 'Gavin - the Senior Cruiser'. Gavin was very elderly and probably would not be able to travel for many more years, but he loved his time aboard.

We were allocated his table in the dining room and I sat next to him. Gavin was almost totally blind, so one of my duties was to read the menu to him each day and help him choose his meal. I made sure he was able to use the condiments and generally made sure he got through the meal without mishap. He had fascinating stories and was endlessly amusing – a great table companion. Gavin loved the quizzes among the other daily entertainment, as he did not take part in the shore excursions.

On the odd occasion when Peter and I did a quiz, we could see Gavin across the room with a small dedicated team of determined quizzers. He always won; there were two quizzes a day and he would win each time. The *Bounty* had a different system of prizes. For each time you won any sport on board you were given a point. You collected up your points and at the end of the cruise you could pick prizes to the value of your points. All the prizes were company logo articles - bookmark, pen, key ring, luggage label, manicure set, umbrella and so on. Gavin greedily collected his points, at least two every day (he occasionally did more than just the quiz) until the last day of this particular cruise, when he swapped the points for prizes. He won an umbrella - a huge golfing umbrella with the Beeline logo on alternate segments. Later, at dinner, he told us he would give it to his sister for her birthday, and I asked him what the secret was to his knowing so much general knowledge.

'I've been on here so long that they have been through the quiz book several times and I know all the answers,' he said. 'Different staff members do the quiz each day and the staff change completely every so often, so they haven't realized yet. I buy all my birthday and Christmas presents with my points. I enjoy the shopping.' His sightless eyes twinkled.

Sadly, I doubt that Gavin is still with us, but wherever he is I am sure he is still quizzing. I hope the quiz book is a thin one and that he can still shop with all his points.

60

OF SARDINES, SNAPPERS AND A GREAT WHITE SHARK

Baltic cruises are wonderful, and our highlight is St Petersburg. There is so much to see in this incredible city, but our favourites are the Hermitage, the Peterhof and the Catherine Palace. On this particular day we were doing the Peterhof in style. We travelled down the river Neva on a hydrofoil to arrive at the landing stage at the bottom of the great staircase up to the palace to see the fountains on each side, setting off the white staircase and the canal within them. We would have an amazing view of the newly-refurbished blue, white and gold decorations of the building set amidst the beautiful gardens and we would be almost alone round the palace, as our arrival would coincide with opening time. Well, that was the plan.

We woke to a grey, grey day with the rain hammering down onto a grey, grey river Neva. The horizons closed in and we could just about see the banks on each side. We had a running commentary from a very knowledgeable young male Russian guide as we made our way to the palace and we concentrated furiously, trying to see or imagine the subjects of the talk. Dressed in our cagoules and by now dripping, we arrived at the landing stage, were disgorged and the hydrofoil left, leaving us stranded.

The landing stage was designed to hold about twenty people comfortably, but there were fifty of us, all dripping on each other. We stood in the pouring rain looking up at the steps before us. It was 10.30, the time we were supposed to arrive and the time the Peterhof opened, but the gate allowing us entry was definitely locked; not just locked, but guarded by two very burly guards. Fifty of us looked at the guards, the guards looked back at us. They did not smile, they did not speak; their eyes appeared dead. They stood in the rain like two huge monoliths doing nothing. We waited until 10.45, when they unlocked the gate and let us enter.

We began to ascend, but no fountains greeted us. We walked a little further and heard a noise behind us; the fountains were switching on in turn behind us. As we passed each pair of fountains, they erupted into life. We stopped, but the guards (now also behind us) were having none of it. They still said nothing, but they made such an effective barrier across the steps that we couldn't stop. We were frogmarched from behind to the entrance to the Peterhof at the top. We waited again, still dripping, at the door while our escorts disappeared, still without a word.

We waited in the downpour another few minutes and began to comment on the lack of welcome. As luck would have it, Peter and I were at the front of the group when suddenly, the door opened to reveal a massive Russian lady (well, we think she was a lady, but she could have been a man) completely filling the space left by the opened door. Standing there, her hands on her hips and a key ring full of jingling keys at what in most people would have been a waist, she was the typical KGB operative. Imagine Rosa Klebb from 'From Russia with Love' (the diminutive poisonous creature with flick knives in the toes of her very sensible lace-up shoes) and multiply her by three and you have some idea of the size of this androgynous leviathan.

'You haff bag,' she shouted, looking straight at me. I held up my front-back pack obediently. She looked furious. 'No, big bag,' she shouted.

I shrugged. 'It's as big as I need,' I said a bit tetchily.

'No, bin, BIN bag,' she shouted again, 'Bin bag for umbrellas.'

I struck the heel of my hand against my forehead, Greek tragedy fashion,

'I knew I had forgotten something! Just fancy me forgetting the bin bag to put our umbrellas in, just in case it rained when we visited Russia,' I said, the sarcasm dripping as heavily as the rain. I turned to everyone else. 'I presume no one has a bin bag they just happen to have brought with them, have they?'

Forty-nine heads shook; no they hadn't. I turned back to Rosa-times-three.

'We don't have bin bags,' I said. 'We are soaking wet and we have the umbrellas, if you want to use them you should have the bin bags. We were supposed to be let in at 10.30, hurry up.' I stared at her truculently right between the eyes, defiantly daring her to shout again. She didn't. She stood back and let us in.

We entered a room which was about eight metres square. In the middle was a movable metal coat rack of the type you see everywhere. All the way round the coat rack was a waist-high wooden barrier with a counter top, leaving a corridor about a metre wide around the room. Diametrically opposite to the door in which we had entered was another door. Our guide (formerly at the back) came to the front, giving me a wide berth. Addressing Peter and the group, he told us we would be making for the door diametrically opposed to the one we were entering by, and he pointed it out to us, and told us that meanwhile we should take off our wet coats and hand them in, over the low barrier which blocked off two ladies and the coat rack in the middle of the room, each coat in exchange for a raffle ticket. We obeyed, and coats disappeared haphazardly onto the movable coat rack in exchange for the tickets. No thought was given to how easy it would be to find the coats when it came to giving them back.

Peter and I gave in our cagoules, and we all shuffled round the narrow corridor at the front of the coat rack. As we arrived at the side of the rack, we saw before us on the floor a shut coffer. Our guide opened it reverently, just as Rosa-times-three shouted, 'SLEEPERS!'

The guide held out the contents of the coffer; pairs of blue plastic overshoes, mostly with the elastic ineffective. We all had to cover our shoes, shoving the plastic inside the tops of our shoes in order to keep them from parting company with us the moment we started walking.

Eventually we were all ready and our guide began to move off with us all in tow. We had gone about six steps when Rosa-times-three was off again. 'COATS!' she screamed at the top of her voice. We continued walking, as we had all taken off our coats, but she was not satisfied. She came charging up behind us, facing Peter and me. She pointed at us.

'Coats,' she yelled.'Offffff!'

Peter had had enough. We were now wearing our leather jackets, which were dry, having originally been under our cagoules, and neither of us was about to remove anything more. 'We have taken off our coats,' he said. 'These are not our coats. We are not taking off anything else.' He gave her the Scott stare. She was flummoxed and walked away, mute.

Our guide looked terrified. 'You must take off your coats,' he whispered.

'We have,' whispered back Peter. Clearly our guide was intimidated by huge Rosa-times-three, but we were not. He nodded and said 'Okay'. Then he led us to our first room and the most incredible floor ever. No wonder they wanted us to wear overslippers.

We enjoyed a spectacular morning exploring the Peterhof. Every corner, wall, ceiling and floor was incredible. The furniture was breathtaking, the doors and windows were intricately worked and the gardens outside were inviting. What a visit, and such a shame it came to an end so quickly.

By the time it was over and we returned for our wet coats, the entrance hall was packed, but only on two sides. Hundreds of people were coming into the palace and only a few were going out, but we were all using the same narrow corridor down two of the sides of the small hall, to and from the only two doors in use, leaving the other two sides of the room outside the barrier completely empty.

'Just barge through and give in your tickets,' our guide had instructed us. 'You have precedence and they will pass the coats back to you over the heads of those coming in.' Easier said than done; no one wanted us to barge through. Logical thought took over, and I addressed Peter, who was by my side. 'How stupid,' I muttered. 'If they used the south and east sides of the room for those coming in, with one person on the front of the coat stand putting the coats up in numerical order, they could use the north and west sides for those going out with another person on the back of the stand giving out the coats. There would be no fuss as they would know exactly where the coats were by the number.'

Peter nodded. If I hadn't said it, he would have.

The guide again told the group to hand over our raffle tickets. We were just about to do this when several of us were accosted by those entering the palace. The coffer of 'sleepers' was now empty. Just a few odd bits of blue plastic were left on the floor to be trodden on and ignored, but people coming in had to wear something on their feet, and in order not to take too long and get left behind by their group, they wanted our 'sleepers'. We balanced on first one leg and then the other, stripping them off and giving them away, or having them snatched by grateful but frustrated tourists.

Rosa-times-three was still shouting, it was still pouring with rain, no bin bag for the umbrellas was to be had anywhere and bedlam reigned. Taking a deep breath, I relinquished my raffle ticket (doubting I would ever see my cagoule again) to the tourist nearest to the low barrier for him to pass it on to the attendants. Tickets went in one direction, coats (still wet) came in the other, all over all our heads. Shouts of 'That's mine!' were heard, and then, 'no, not that one, that one,' as no one knew which person went with which coat. I could have sworn I heard a shout of 'Put me down, it's mine and I'm still wearing it.'

Jackets and macs went up and down the crowd, passing from one uplifted hand to another, while coats coming in from those entering were at a dead stop. The ballet of the coats went on for several anxious minutes. Peter and I recovered our cagoules, but there was no chance of slipping them on as there simply wasn't room to stretch out our arms; arms could only go in one direction, upwards.

The coats kept coming, the coats slowed down, the coats eventually stopped. Our guide had already given instructions that as soon as we had our coats we were to meet outside in the gardens. We pushed through the scrum of tourists waiting to leave their outer garments. At last we popped out like champagne corks through the door marked 'exit' on the inside and 'entrance' on the outside, popping out a few people who didn't want to be popped out on the way.

We all stood, breathed (I think most of us had held our breath during the dance of the coats) and took stock. A quick trip round the very wet gardens and we were driven off in a coach, this time to return to the ship via the other high spots of the city.

I wonder if they still use just two sides of that room, or if it has been pointed out that a one-way system is a much easier way?

Now, far be it from me to tell you how to do your holiday packing, but once you have your toothbrush, perhaps thought should be given to your bin bag; you just never know when it might come in handy. Of course, you have to keep it handy at all times to ensure it does come in handy, but in rainy Russia, well, if Russian brownie points are your thing, this could be the tip of a lifetime.

61

EXODUS

In her eyes, Mum was never wrong. When she failed one of her several driving tests for knocking out the nearside headlight by hitting a tree during a three-point turn she could not understand what the fuss was about, or why she had failed. 'It wasn't my fault,' was how she put it. As she was never wrong, she had no coping strategies for when the elements conspired against her.

We were in Norway. Mum had been in the coffee shop, which was inside a visitors' centre, while we were admiring a view, or a glacier, or a waterfall, I don't remember exactly which, or it might have been all three. She was going to meet us at the bus which was standing immediately across the road from the centre. We arrived at the bus first, so we waited for Mum outside, in the layby.

The visitors' centre had an automatic glass door. It was the sliding variety, so the whole of the door slid across a fixed piece of glass. You could work it manually by pressing a pad on a small pillar outside, or another on the wall inside. It was busy on this particular day, so there was no need to do anything manually; the door was sliding open and shut more or less continually as people walked through.

There were a few clues as to which was the door and which the immovable glass. The door had ENTRANCE on the outside in very large letters. We assume it had EXIT on the inside in the same sort of letters, as everyone seemed to be exiting that way. There was also a welcome mat inside the door, only they aren't welcome mats really, are they? They are wipe-your-shoes-before-you-come-in-because-they-are-bound-to-be-dirty mats, and this one was the width of the door. The biggest clue of all, though, was that people were walking through the door all the time; they were not walking through the fixed glass, to which were attached one or two silhouettes of raptors.

Mum saw us through the glass and waved. She then walked to the door, except that she didn't. She actually walked to the fixed piece of glass and tried walking through it. It didn't work. She was firmly rebutted by the glass. She tried again, and again she was denied exit. It was at this point that Mum's total lack of problem-solving strategy came into force. She went into wasp mode, and ran at the fixed glass. We have all seen it; a wasp or a house fly will fly at a window, seeing the outside outside and presuming they can fly to it, and when they can't, they just fly a bit faster and harder and still get nowhere. They batter themselves against the window – they don't give up, if you had time, you could probably watch them for hours, but you either open the window, swat them or leave them.

Mum was just the same; she started hurling herself at the window, then she handbagged it and we could see she started shouting. Alas, she just didn't have the ability of Harry Potter at King's Cross Station; she was only a muggle.

Meanwhile, people were walking in and out of the door, not noticing anything. As we waited, some of the other passengers joined us and an interested group watched her antics. By this time, we were signalling at Mum to move to her right to exit. Several others joined in. Mum just went on throwing herself at the window, finally spreadeagling herself across the glass like a flattened insect.

'I'll have to go and rescue her,' said Peter, and he jogged off over the roadway. They came back together.

'They ought to move that door,' said Mum.

An environmentally friendly book printed and bound in England by www.printondemand-worldwide.com

PEFC Certified

This product is from sustainably managed forests and controlled sources

www.pefc.org

MIX
Paper from responsible sources
FSC® C004959

This book is made entirely of sustainable materials; FSC paper for the cover and PEFC paper for the text pages

Reprint of # - C0 - 203/127/24 - PB - Lamination Gloss - Printed on 22-May-17 10:47